JUSTICE

JUSTICE

Louis P. Pojman
Cambridge University

Upper Saddle River, New Jersey 07458

Library of Congress Cataloging-in-Publication Data

Pojman, Louis P.
  Justice / Louis P. Pojman.
    p. cm.
  Includes bibliographical references and index.
  ISBN 0-13-183515-7 (alk. paper)
  1. Justice. 1. Title.
  JC578.P64 2004
  340'.11—dc22

                      2004062529

Editorial Director: Charlyce Jones Owen
Editorial Assistant: Carla Worner
Assistant Editor: Wendy Yurash
Marketing Manager: Kara Kindstrom
Marketing Assistant: Jennifer Lang
Managing Editor: Joanne Riker
Production Liaison: Fran Russello
Manufacturing Buyer: Christina Helder
Art Director: Jayne Conte
Cover Design: Kiwi Design
Composition/Full-Service Project Management: GGS Book Services,
  Atlantic Highlands
Printer/Binder: Phoenix Book Tech Park
Cover Printer: Phoenix Book Tech Park

Credits and acknowledgments borrowed from other sources and reproduced, with permission, in this textbook appear on appropriate page within text.

Pearson Education LTD. London
Pearson Education Singapore, Pte. Ltd
Pearson Education, Canada, Ltd
Pearson Education–Japan
Pearson Education Australia PTY, Limited

Pearson Education North Asia Ltd
Pearson Educación de Mexico, S.A. de C.V.
Pearson Education Malaysia, Pte. Ltd
Pearson Education, Upper Saddle River,
  New Jersey

10 9 8 7 6 5 4 3 2 1

ISBN: 0-13-183515-7

Dedicated to the memory of My Teachers
Reinhold Niebuhr (1892–1971)
and
Richard M. Hare (1919–2001)

Contents

Preface

> I hate, I despise your feasts,
> and I take no delight in your solemn assemblies.
> Even though you offer me your burnt offerings and cereal
> offerings, I will not accept them,
> and the peace offerings of your fatted beasts
> I will not look upon.
> Take away from me the noise of your songs;
> to the melody of your harps I will not listen.
> But let justice roll down like waters,
> and righteousness like an ever-flowing stream.
>
> (Amos 5:22–24)

> Remove justice, and what are kingdoms but gangs of criminals on a large scale.
> (Augustine, *City of God*)

"Justice," John Rawls has written, "is the first virtue of social institutions, as truth is of systems of thought." But as Rawls also notes, although justice is the most important concept in political philosophy, it is also one of the most contested concepts in philosophy. Justice is not the only social-political value, and those who take an absolutist line (*fiat justicia ruat caelum*—"let there be justice even if the heaven falls") are mistaken. But justice is of vital importance and merits our comprehensive attention. The concept is a systematically contested one that is tossed about rhetorically from many quarters. A plethora of confusing, competing theories abound, so that one needs a road map to find one's way about. I have tried to provide a philosophical map of the terrain in order to help in that endeavor.

I begin in Chapter 1 with an Introduction, giving an overview of the concept of justice and arguing that justice is a vital part of political philosophy, which in turn is part of moral philosophy. As such, I outline an objectivist view of moral philosophy, which holds that moral principles have universal validity. Morality is the most important institution for social life, and politics is a function of morality. I distinguish between formal and material concepts of justice and discuss the related issues of comparative/noncomparative justice and distributive versus commutative justice. In Chapter 2 I outline the classic desert theory of justice. In Chapter 3 I examine the libertarian concept of justice in the work of Robert Nozick. In Chapter 4 I discuss the most prominent liberal theories, those of the late John Rawls. In Chapter 5 I look at recent pluralist theories of justice, develop my own version of these theories, and show how they can be consistent with objectivist theories. In Chapter 6, I examine the idea of equal opportunity, arguing that while the concept of equal opportunity is ambiguous, it is the most plausible candidate for a lineage between equality and justice. In Chapter 7 I outline and defend a cosmopolitan view of justice. (The idea of universality set forth in Chapter 1 has implications leading to moral and political cosmopolitanism.) Finally, in Chapter 8 I consider criminal justice, especially retributive justice, and argue for a pluralist version of penal justice.

I have tried to be impartial and fair in assessing various theories in this work, but nevertheless my own conclusions are often clearly stated.

I am grateful to Ross Miller, the Philosophy Editor of Prentice-Hall, for the opportunity to write this book and for his strong support during the writing process. This book is dedicated to the memory of two of my teachers who greatly influenced my early thinking on moral and political philosophy, Reinhold Niebuhr and Richard Hare. This book was written while teaching a Political Philosophy class at West Point. I am profoundly indebted to the cadets in that class who offered trenchant criticisms of my theses and often helped me reformulate my arguments. The members of the class were: Margot Alexander, Andrew Canfield, Joshua Conary, Michael Daschle, Mark Davis, Shay Finley, Michael Harper, Katherine Heine, Phillip Hensel, Peter Kuzma, Peter Lawall, William Mariani, Chris Pestel, and Jonathan Stone.

William Cornwell, Gary Foulk, Jonathan Harrison, Tony Hartle, Stephen Kershnar, Sterling Harwood, Joe Miller, Peter Tramel, and members of the English and Philosophy Department at West Point offered constructive criticisms on many of the chapters in this work. I am also grateful to the reviewers of this manuscript: Michael Green, University of Chicago; Choong Lee, University of South Carolina–Spartanburg; and Stephen Kershnar, SUNY–Fredonia. Most of all I am indebted to my wife, Trudy, who has been my best friend and my most supportive and critical reader.

Louis P. Pojman
Clare Hall
Cambridge University
October 26, 2004

JUSTICE

CHAPTER 1

Introduction

> Justice, [Aristotle] said, consists in treating equals equally and unequals unequally, but in proportion to their relevant differences. This involves, first, the idea of impartiality. . . . Impartiality implies a kind of equality—not that all cases should be treated alike but that the onus rests on whoever would treat them differently to distinguish them in relevant ways. . . . That is what is really meant by the right to equal consideration—to be treated alike unless relevant differences have been proved.
>
> (Stanley Benn, *Encyclopedia of Philosophy*)

> It is only from the selfishness and confined generosity of men, along with the scanty provision nature has made for his wants, that justice derives its origin.
>
> (David Hume, *A Treatise of Human Nature*, Oxford University Press, 1739)

The Circumstances of Justice

Problems of justice arise, as David Hume pointed out over two centuries ago, when in situations of scarcity we, creatures of limited sympathies, seek to adjudicate between competing claims for limited goods.[1] Hume refers to this as the "circumstances of justice." If either we were complete altruists or if goods were unlimited, questions of justice would not arise. If we had unlimited sympathies, property would not exist, and no distinctions between *mine* and *thine* would obtain. If you needed the house I built, I would share it with you or move out. If your child needed the food in my garden, she would be free to take it, and similarly, my child would help himself to the food you had grown. Likewise, if there were unlimited resources, we would not worry about distribution of goods. If you wanted a car like mine, you would pick one out from the innumerable ones readily available. No competition for jobs or resources would be necessary, because there would be plenty of everything for everyone. This may be a description of heaven, but it is not our world. Neither ideal condition obtains. We are not complete altruists, nor are resources unlimited, but the very opposite. Consider this example: Suppose one hundred candidates apply for a highly desirable position (e.g., quarterback for a professional football team, university professorship, position of chief surgeon in a medical center, airline pilot or CEO), but only one position is available. What are the correct moral and legal criteria by which to decide who should get the job? Should the selection be based on merit, individual need, utility, previous effort, likely contribution to be made, or should the decision be left to market forces, giving the hiring group complete discretion in making its choice? Should race, ethnicity and gender be taken into consideration? If in the past blacks and women or the disabled have been systematically discriminated against, should affirmative action programs engaging in reverse discrimination be utilized, showing favor to less qualified women and blacks over more qualified white males (who themselves, though innocent of wrongdoing, may have profited from past favoritism)? Or consider the use of kidney dialysis machines in a county hospital that can afford only 5 machines, but has a waiting list of 20 or 30 people. How should we decide which five should be treated? by lottery? by a process of first come-first served? by greatest need? by merit? by desert? by utility? (For example, one of the candidates is the mayor of one of the towns who has served the community well for many years.) Or should a complex set of factors (including age, contribution, responsibilities, merit, and need) be used? Should equal work be rewarded with equal pay, or should the matter be left entirely to the discretion of the employer or what the market will bear?

The most significant and debated issue in the debate over distributive justice is that of economic justice. There are great discrepancies between the rich and poor. What, if anything, should we do about them? Consider the 18th century Utilitarian, William Paley's Parable of the Pigeons:

> If you should see a flock of pigeons in a field of corn and if (instead of each pecking where, and what it liked, taking just as much as it wanted, and no more) you should see ninety-nine of them gathering all they got into a heap; reserving nothing for themselves, but the chaff and refuse; keeping this heap for one, and that the weakest perhaps and worst pigeon of the flock; sitting round, and looking on, all the winter, while this one was devouring, throwing about and wasting it; and, if a pigeon more hardy or hungry than the rest, touched a grain of the hoard, all the others instantly flying upon it, and tearing it to pieces; if you should see this, you would see nothing more, than what is every day practiced and established among men. Among men you see the ninety and nine, toiling and scraping together a heap of superfluities for one; getting nothing for themselves all the while, but a little of the coarsest of the provisions; and this one too, often the feeblest and worst of the whole set, a child, a woman, a madman, or a fool; looking quietly on, while they see the fruits of all their labor spent or spoiled; and if one of them take or touch a particle of it, the others join against him, and hang him for the theft.[2]

The Allegory of Paley's Pigeons seems to be exemplified in modern society. Professional athletes and entertainers often make millions of dollars a year, more than school teachers or nurses will make in a lifetime of dedicated service. The highest paid federal employee is not the president of the United States or the chairman of the joint Chiefs of Staff, but the football coach of the Air Force Academy. Football players and coaches make more than Supreme Court justices or the president of the United States. What may be even more galling are the idle rich, who have inherited great fortunes and live in the lap of luxury, while the poor don't have enough to eat or adequate shelter. It is not just the enormous gap between rich and poor that upsets many of us, but the lack of social responsibility manifest by Paley's contemporary pigeons as they flaunt their jewelry, fast cars, and Beverly Hills mansions.

We may ask, then, Is something unjust about the discrepancy between the salaries of baseball stars and public school teachers? Which vocation is more important for society, being a baseball player or a teacher? If the nurturing and education of children is a higher priority than professional football or baseball, does justice require that this fact be reflected in our economic rewards?

Justice and Moral Philosophy

Over two millennia ago Plato in *The Republic* asked, "What is Justice?" This question in his classical treatise inaugurated the discipline of political philosophy in which the question of justice still remains the fundamental question.

Justice is part of normative Political Philosophy, which in turn is part of Moral Philosophy. It is significant that the same Greek word, *dikaiosune*, which Plato uses for "justice" also means "morally righteous." Moral Philosophy has certain constituent features that include universality, prescriptivity, and impartiality. (1) The *principle of universality* states that morality is universal, applying to all people everywhere. A core set of principles are binding on every human being regardless of culture, race, or gender. Perhaps there are some moral rules specific to culture, rules that moral philosophy would judge as optional, but a core set seems constitutive of every human society, principles such as respecting human life, safeguarding individual freedom, protecting property, not causing unnecessary suffering, and promise keeping.[3] Justice seems to have an objective core; however, like all moral principles it differs in its contextual application. Law is the institutional product of morality, an attempt to codify morality in a system of general rules that are enforced and surrounded with sanctions, but there can be unjust and immoral laws, such as laws promoting slavery and oppression of women. If ethical relativism were true, the phrase *immoral law* would be an oxymoron (a contradiction in terms) since morality just is what the culture decides. But it is more reasonable to hold that an objective, universal morality does exist and underlies ideal law.

(2) The *principle of prescriptivity* means that moral principles are not merely descriptions of states of affairs in the world, but are normative. They tell us what *ought* to be the case, even if it is not likely that such an ideal will be realized.

(3) The *principle of impartiality* or *universalizability*, is purely formal (see below under *formal justice*) and tells us that whatever principles we adopt, they must be applied impartially, without regard to accidental features, such as race, gender, religion, or social or economic class. As Stanley Benn writes, "Impartiality implies a kind of equality—not that all cases should be treated alike but that the onus rests on whoever would treat them differently to distinguish them in relevant ways."

(See the epigraph at the head of this chapter.) Impartiality is often confused with *neutrality*, but they are opposites. Consider a football game, say between arch rivals such as the University of Notre Dame and the University of Michigan. The peanut vendor from California, who hates football and couldn't care less who wins the game is neutral between the teams. The fans are the paradigm of partiality, rooting for their teams like religious fanatics. But the paradigm of impartiality is the umpire, who knowing his wife has just bet their pension funds on the under-dog, still manages to call a fair game, making correct calls even in relatively ambiguous situations. Impartiality is not neutrality or indifference. It is, rather, making judgments according to rules. As such, morality involves taking sides in disputes, doing so according to the approved set of rules. These rules may include special obligations, giving special consideration to one's family and friends, to whom we have special relations. Justice as impartiality requires that professionals, such as physicians and lawyers, serve their clients whether or not they like them, treating them according to the rules of the profession, not according to their race, religion, facial appearance, or family background.

These are the main formal features of morality. There are probably others, but they are more controversial, such as *publicity* and *practicality* (ought implies can), but the three described seem most central.

To sum up, morality, in part at least, must be objectively valid, applying to all people everywhere; otherwise we could not discuss justice as a universal concept, but simply speak of it as relative only to a given society. Here is one example that illustrates the difference that one's view of the universality of morality makes. It is the case of a girl from Mali, named Seba. Here is her story:

I was raised by my grandmother in Mali, and when I was still a little girl a woman my family knew came and asked her if she could take me to Paris to care for her children. She told my grandmother that she would put me in school, and that I would learn French. But when I came to Paris I was not sent to school. I had to work every day. In her house I did all the work; I cleaned the house, cooked the meals, cared for the children, and washed and fed the baby. Every day I started work before 7 AM and finished about 11 PM; I never had a day off. My mistress did nothing; she slept late and then watched televi-sion or went out.

One day I told her that I wanted to go to school. She replied that she had not brought me to France to go to school but to take care of her children. I was so tired and run down. I had problems with my teeth; sometimes my cheek would swell and the pain would be terrible. Sometimes I had stom-achaches, but when I was ill I still had to work. Sometimes when I was in pain I would cry, but my mistress would shout at me.

. . . She would often beat me. She would slap me all the time. She beat me with a broom, with kitchen tools, or whipped me with electric cable. Sometimes I would bleed; I still have marks on my body.

Once in 1992, I was late going to get the children from school; my mistress and her husband were furious with me and beat me and then threw me out on the street. I didn't understand anything, and I wandered on the street. After some time her husband found me and took me back to the house. There they stripped me naked, tied my hands behind my back, and began to whip me with a wire attached to a broomstick. Both of them were beating me at the same time. I was bleeding a lot and screaming, but they continued to beat me. Then she rubbed chili pepper into my wounds and stuck it in my vagina. I lost consciousness.[4]

Surely, this case of modern slavery is an instance of injustice. Seba was treated with malicious cruelty. What happened to Seba should not happen to a dog, let alone a little girl. It is morally wrong, even if the people who enslaved Seba believed what they were doing was morally permissible. You can be sincere but mistaken. It is immoral to cause unnecessary suffering; furthermore, it is not only immoral, but a specific type of immorality. It is unjust. Put yourself in Seba's shoes. Would you like to be treated this way?

If, as I have suggested above, morality is universally objective, and respecting liberty is one constitutive feature of morality, then slavery such as endured by Seba is wrong, whether or not a culture approves of it.[5]

Justice is a moral-political value, but it is not the only moral-political value. Liberty, integrity, benevolence, and utility are also political values with a moral core. Liberty is valuable since we all value freedom as one of the necessary conditions for a good life. People like Seba, who live as virtual slaves, cannot live an adequately fulfilled life; they cannot exercise autonomy. We want to live our lives in our own way, in a manner that seems best to us. We prize freedom of thought, freedom of movement, freedom of speech, and freedom of worship as fundamental to a well-organized state. Similarly, we value utility. A society and state ought to promote a high total and average level of welfare or utility. Under utility is the concept of efficiency. We want effective and efficient institutions. A program that generally meets needs, generally renders justice and welfare, but takes forever to do so, is defective. We deserve better.

The medieval Catholic philosopher, Thomas Aquinas, defined law as consisting in the standards of justice which exist for the common good of the community and should be compulsory.[6] Justice differs from other parts of morality in that it covers aspects of morality that we may be compelled to perform under threat of punishment. It is morally good to devote substantial amounts of time to helping the poor and volunteering for community service, but no one has a right to compel us to do so. But the state or the community should compel us to refrain from murder or from enslaving people. Altruism may be supererogatory, a virtue that we may encourage but not command, but the rules of justice can and should be commanded, for justice forms the content of those rules that are necessary for living a minimally decent life in a community.

At the most fundamental level justice arises in order to stave off a state of nature, described by Thomas Hobbes (1588–1679) as a "war of all against all," where no one is secure, but life is "solitary, poor, nasty, brutish, and short."[7] In order to prevent this dismal predicament, reason tells us to follow certain rules, including "the first law," seeking peace, foregoing the use of violence, and "the second law," claiming no more liberty against your neighbor than you would be willing to allow your neighbor against you. The third law of nature is "Keep Covenants Made." For a society to work, agreements must be strictly adhered to. Hobbes saw the social contract as the entire essence of justice. At the heart of justice is the protection of our liberty, our right to do what we please, to live life as we wish, as long as we are not unjustly harming other people. For Hobbes distributive justice consists entirely in what we agree with others to do. As long as agreements are uncoerced, they are just and demand our adherence. Hobbes provides us with a starting point to discuss justice, but justice may include more than simply keeping covenants. First of all, as David Hume (1711–1776) pointed out, there never was such an historic social contract, and even if there was, why should we, who were not part of the original agreement, continue to adhere to its rules. We can defend part of Hobbes's thesis against Hume by arguing that the minimal content of Hobbes's thought experiment is set forth for our mutual advantage. Without the rules of minimal morality, life would probably be "solitary, poor, nasty, brutish, and short." But it seems that justice, while not determining the entire content of morality, involves more than protecting our right to life and adherence to contract. It seems to cover the whole gamut of distributing benefits and burdens in society.

Formal and Material Principles of Justice

Theories of justice may be divided into formal and material types. A formal theory of justice provides the formula or definition of justice without directly filling in the content or criteria of application. Material theories of justice specify the relevant content to be inserted into the formulas. They tell us what the relevant criterion is.

The classical principle of formal justice, based on Book V of Aristotle's *Nicomachean Ethics*, is that "equals should be treated equally and unequals unequally." The formula is one of proportionality:

$$\frac{A \text{ has } X \text{ of } P}{B \text{ has } Y \text{ of } P} = \frac{A \text{ should have } X \text{ of } Q \text{ [put} = \text{sign]}}{B \text{ should have } Y \text{ of } Q}$$

That is, if person A has X units of a relevant property (P), and B has Y units (where Y is more or less than X), then A should receive proportionally more or less of the relevant reward or good (Q) than B. If A has worked eight hours at a job and B only four hours, and working time is the relevant criterion of reward, then A should be paid twice as much as B.

The formal principle is used in law in the guise of *stare decisis*, the rule of precedent—like cases should be decided in like manner. The principle applies not only to the case of distributive justice, but also the case of *retributive* (punishment—"an eye for an eye, a tooth for a tooth, a life for a life") and *commutative* justice, in which obligation is based on a promise or contract that requires fulfillment. In Chapters 1 to 4 of the present work, we will concentrate on the central type of justice, distributive, but in Chapter 8 we will deal with retributive justice under the general issue of punishment.

The formal principle of justice seems reducible to the principle of universalizability (discussed above): treat like cases similarly unless there is a relevant difference, which itself is simply the principle of consistency. Be consistent in your decisions. If you can't find a relevant difference between agents, treat them similarly (e.g., what's good for the goose is good for the gander). If it's alright for boys to engage in premarital sex, then it's alright for girls to do so too, since there is no relevant moral difference between the genders.

Some philosophers, such as Stanley Benn, believe that the formal principle of justice, involving equal treatment for equals and unequal treatment for unequals, is a kind of impartiality, implying a kind of *presumption* of equal treatment of people. We should generally treat everyone alike, until it is shown that a relevant difference exists between them. But there are problems with this viewpoint.

Sometimes the presumption should be, not for equal treatment, but instead, for unequal treatment of people. Suppose that a father suddenly decides to share his fortune, and he divides it in two and gives half each to his oldest son and his neighbor's oldest son.[8] We should say that this kind of equality is misguided and, in fact, unjust. We need to specify the respect in which people are equal and so deserve the same kind of treatment, and this seems to be a material problem, not a purely formal one.

The formal principle of justice doesn't tell us whether some act is right or wrong; it simply calls for consistency. If we were content to live only with the formal principle, we might treat people very badly, and as long as we were consistent, be considered just. As one of his players once said of the famous coach of football's Green Bay Packers, Vince Lombardi, "He treated us all equally—like dogs."

The formal principle does not tell us which qualities, distribution of goods or treatment, there should be. Thus, a material principle is needed to supplement or fill in the formal principle. Aristotle's own principle was merit. People should be treated according to their merit or abilities, people who were equally meritorious should be treated equally, and unequally from those who were less or more meritorious than they. So a football coach could only justly treat his players like dogs if they really were doglike. Otherwise, he would be enjoined to treat them differently, more humanely. Other candidates for material principles of justice are need, equality, rights, and desert. We shall examine theories based on these principles in the next two chapters.

As long as a relevant difference is identified, formal equality can endorse different treatments. The U.S. Supreme Court has ruled that gender sometimes constitutes a relevant difference in application of the law. Noting biological differences in *Schlesinger v. Ballard*, it upheld differential tenure rules of male and female naval officers, ruling that women are entitled to a longer period of service before mandatory discharge for want of promotion goes into effect. This seems reasonable, based on the probability that women will take time off to give birth and nurture their children. So it seems that the formal principle of justice lacks substantive content.

Material theories of justice may be further divided into patterned and nonpatterned types of justice. A patterned principle chooses some trait(s) that indicates how the proper distribution is to be accomplished. It has the form:

To each according to _____:

In his *Anarchy, State, and Utopia*, Robert Nozick puts the matter this way, "Let us call a principle of distribution *patterned* if it specifies that a distribution is to vary along with some natural dimension, weighted sum of natural dimensions, or lexicographic ordering of natural dimensions." Nozick rejects patterned types of principles, such as those of Aristotle, meritocrats, socialists, and egalitarians because such an attempt to regulate distribution constitutes a violation of liberty.

Most theories of justice are the patterned variety, illustrated by the symbol of Lady Justice, the blindfolded woman, holding a pair of equally balanced scales in her hand, the metaphor pointing to the absolute symmetry between the quality of the human actions on the right side and the rewards or punishments on the left side. Justice is blind to all irrelevant considerations such as birth or social status or race or gender; it is concerned only with giving one what he or she deserves.

This work is intended to be an exploration into the concept of justice, and not the last word on the subject. As I have mentioned, I presuppose an objectivist view of ethics; otherwise it makes no sense to speak of a correct principle of justice. Justice would be relative to a culture, not simply contextual to various situations. My analysis is compatible with both consequentialist theories, such as utilitarianism, and deontological ones, such as Kantian theories. We will analyze the theory of justice as desert in the next chapter. But first we should examine some further preliminary issues, beginning with whether justice is comparative or noncomparative.

Is Justice Comparative or Noncomparative?

Joel Feinberg has argued that the paradigm of justice is noncomparative—simply getting what one deserves. Most cases are simply geared to the individual's quality, though there are exceptions, such as awarding a prize to the first person to cross the finish line in a race (we can compare him with the other runners) or grading on a curve (where we differentiate between students on the basis of increments). Similarly, egregiously cruel punishment is more unjust in comparison to less cruel punishment. Phillip Montague, on the other hand, has argued that justice is solely noncomparative and that Feinberg's examples of comparative justice can be assimilated into a noncomparative theory: in a race, the victorious runner can be described comparatively as coming in first, but also noncomparatively, as the *winner*, and so noncomparatively deserves the prize; even when grades are given on a preformulated curve, the students in a given percentile noncomparatively deserve the grade agreed upon by the system of rules. Cruel punishment is noncomparatively unjust, though it may be more evil than less cruel punishment that is still crueler than warranted. Kant would say that each person has a moral quotient to which a level of happiness is fitting. I deserve to be happy in proportion to my moral conscientiousness. Similarly, it seems that it is always unjust to punish the innocent.

Recently, the Polish-Australian philosopher Wojciech Sadurski has taken the opposite position from Feinberg and Montague, contending that all justice distribution is comparative, comparative to class and culture. For example, giving the grade of an A may appear noncomparative, but it will characterize a different quality of work depending on whether we are grading high school, university, graduate, professional essays, or Nobel Prize winners.[9]

There may be a misunderstanding in this debate. Those holding the noncomparative thesis would agree that there is a class of comparison within which we make our appraisals, but that is a meta or higher-order decision. Once we do that preliminary work, judging the relevant class to be high school students or professional philosophers, we can apply a noncomparative standard. So we can divide the field into external and internal considerations and assert that externally comparative criteria apply, but internally they do not.

If we do this, most of our judgments will be noncomparative, but a few, like cruel punishment, will sometimes be comparative. It is unjust to punish someone more severely than the crime warrants (such as torturing or executing people for parking violations or petty theft). Feinberg gives the illustration of Augustine's theory of human depravity. According to Augustine, all humans are sinners and equally undeserving of salvation, but God arbitrarily elects a few to be saved. This seems to be a case of comparative injustice, the saved getting more than they deserve, the damned getting exactly what they deserve. We can imagine that some of the damned are less wicked than others but get equal punishment. That would illustrate another departure from exact justice.

Sometimes "justice" is used as a synonym with "fairness," as is the case with Rawls's theory (which we shall examine in Chapter 4). But these concepts can be distinguished. I had a friend, Jerry, who once complained to me of being treated unjustly in that he received two speeding tickets in one afternoon, while other drivers traveling faster than he apparently were not ticketed at all. Jerry was not treated unjustly, since he admitted he was deserving of the tickets, but, at worst, unfairly, since the police did not treat other speeders the same way. Similarly, in the above example of Augustine's doctrine of election, the damned are not being treated fairly, since the saved are arbitrarily singled out for special treatment. But they are being treated justly, since they are receiving what is their due.

Or suppose you get a C− on your philosophy exam, a grade you richly merit, judged by impartial standards. However, Jane the teacher's pet gets an A for the same quality work. It's not fair that Jane gets a higher grade than you for the same quality exam, but you cannot complain that your grade is unjust. Justice is keyed to objective standards, whereas fairness has to do with consistency of application. Something can be just but unfair or fair but unjust—as would be the case if the teacher gave you both an A for your exams. Rawls wants to collapse the distinction, making fairness synonymous with justice, but this obscures a genuine distinction. Fairness is comparative, while justice typically is noncomparative.

If this is true, Aristotle's formula (p. 6) is really about fairness. It states that if John has twice as much value V as Jill, John should receive twice as much of the reward or punishment as Jill without giving an absolute quantity of the reward or punishment. It offers us a ratio, a proportionate index, but not an answer to the question, "What does John deserve?"

But suppose John and Jill are equally deserving, but John is twice as happy as Jill, who is as happy as she deserves to be. Noncomparative justice would require us to reduce John's quotient, but comparative justice or fairness, being infused with a touch of utilitarianism, might incline us to upgrade Jill's quotient, if we can, to approximate John's. Similarly, suppose John is making twice as much money as Jill, who is making barely enough to survive. Economic justice may not give us an answer to what equally deserving John and Jill absolutely deserve, but fairness would require us to pay both of them an approximately equal living wage, probably closer to John's wage than Jill's. Still, if Jill strikes a deal with her employer to get more than John is getting, no injustice is done to John—as long as he continues to receive a living wage equal to that of most others in the comparative class. But if the average wage of the comparative class rises, leaving John far behind, comparative justice would conclude that John is being treated unjustly. As we will see in Chapter 3 and in the section on commutative justice (below), some philosophers argue that whatever workers and employers agree to is just, regardless of comparative differences.

Law, Justice, and Equity

We mentioned Aquinas's plausible claim that law is the attempt to promote justice in society, to protect vital aspects of morality, those that we often call rights. The problem is that laws are necessarily framed as general rules that apply broadly to a wide range of cases. It generally cannot anticipate all the particular contingencies in life. Hence, as Aristotle wrote, *Equity* is required for the "rectification of law in so far as law is deficient on account of its generality."[10] Aquinas gives the example of a city that has a law requiring that the city's gates be closed at a certain hour each night. Even though the law is reasonable, for it usually serves to protect the city from intruders and invaders, the officials may equitably decree the opening of the gates after closure in order to save soldiers who are fleeing an enemy. Similarly, in a modern law court, a judge may admit excusing or supplementary evidence to mitigate the verdict or sentencing of the accused even when he has clearly broken the law. Finally, while the law reasonably requires that all vehicles stop at stop signs or traffic lights, *Equity* permits emergency violations of those laws and allows a driver to run a stop sign (if he judges it to be safe) in order to drive his pregnant-in-labor wife to the hospital in order to give birth to a child.

Justice is impervious of individual preferences, but equity is not. Suppose that John Smith has bequeathed four beautiful gems to his nieces, two of them diamond-shaped and two oval-shaped. Niece A is particularly fond of diamond-shaped gems, whereas niece B prefers oval-shaped. In allocating the gems to each niece, there are three possibilities:

1. Each niece gets one of each type.
2. Both diamond-shaped gems go to A, the others to B.
3. Both oval-shaped gems go to A, the others to B.

The fair distribution seems to be (1), which treats the two parties in an equal manner even though both nieces would prefer (2). Since John wants to act justly, he would choose distribution (1) and allow the nieces to make their trades according to their subjective preferences.[11] If John took the subjective preferences into consideration in making the distribution, he would not be acting unjustly, but *nonjustly*, since no claim of the nieces was being violated. Strict formal justice focuses on objective claims, whereas equity focuses on individual preferences. Equity supplements the law, correcting it in order that it may better serve the spirit of justice.

Commutative Justice

Aristotle distinguished distributive justice from commutative justice. We should note the difference.

There is a famous parable in Matthew's Gospel (chapter 20) of a rich farmer hiring day laborers to harvest his crops. He goes into the marketplace early in the morning and hires an early-bird group of workers to work for a certain fee. They go to work. Later that day the farmer realizes that he needs more laborers, so he goes into the marketplace again and hires another group to work in his field for the rest of the day at the same fee as the original laborers contracted. They go to work. Then late in the afternoon, he goes into the marketplace and hires a third group ("the latecomers") to work for the few remaining hours at the same fee. When the day closes, the farmer pays the workers the agreed-upon wages. The early birds complain that they have worked much longer and accomplished far more than the latecomers and should get paid accordingly. The farmer responds, "I did you no injustice in paying you the wages we agreed upon."

The parable illustrates the difference between *distributive* justice, which entails that equals be treated equally and unequals unequally, and what Aristotle called *commutative* justice, the justice of contracts. As long as contracts are agreed upon freely, they seem fair. Still, we would think that the landlord should have adjusted the wage scale to pay those who worked longer more money. The usual interpretation of this story is that the workers who labored all day received a fair wage, but the landlord was supererogatory or benevolent in paying those who only worked one hour more than they deserved. Perhaps we might conclude that so-called *commutative justice* is really about fairness, not justice.

The parable seems to illustrate not only the difference between commutative and distributive justice, but also the difference between legal and moral justice. As long as the agreement broke no laws, it was legal to pay the latecomers as much as the early workers, but morally, we would be inclined to say an aspect of proportionality has been flaunted. According to distributive justice, equal pay should be paid for equal work and unequal pay for unequal work, but according to *commutative justice* as long as no contract is breeched, the transaction is fair. Libertarians who tend to emphasize this concept of justice argue that as long as the people agree to work for the wages they receive, no exploitation occurs. Those who focus on *distributive* justice argue that if the social conditions are unfavorable, the rich can take advantage of the poor who are desperate, in which case exploitation can occur.

Along these same lines, some people hold that justice means "equality before the law." But this is an ambiguous concept that may mean either "equal enforcement of the existing laws" or "substantive laws which are not based on arbitrary or unfair discrimination" ("equality in law"). With regard to mere equality before the law or equal protection of the law, John Stuart Mill expressed the fundamental problem:

> The justice of giving equal protection to the rights of all, is maintained by those who support the most outrageous inequality in the rights themselves. Even in slave countries it is theoretically admitted that the rights of the slave, such as they are, ought to be as sacred as those of the master; and that a tribunal which fails to enforce them with equal strictness is wanting in justice.

The principle of equality before the law is no more than one of consistency or nonarbitrariness, a formal principle treating equals equally and unequals unequally, but saying nothing about the substantive criterion for making the relevant judgment.

Democracy, Capitalism, and Distributive Justice

Democracy, critics like Plato and De Tocqueville argue, tends to mediocratize—leveling downward, producing equality of conditions at the cost of excellence. Those on the bottom in wealth and status tend to envy those better off, dragging them downwards. As De Tocqueville put it, "There is indeed a manly and legitimate passion for equality which rouses in all men a desire to be strong and respected. This passion tends to elevate the little man to the rank of the great. But the human heart also nourishes a debased taste for equality, which leads the weak to want to drag the strong down to their level and which induces men to prefer equality in servitude to inequality in freedom."[12] Capitalism, however, has the opposite danger, tending to increase inequality, as the rich get richer and the poor poorer. Yet capitalism also tends to promote economic incentive, creating overall wealth. Since a rising tide lifts all boats, the general direction is toward greater wealth, even though great inequalities accompany that aggregate wealth.[13] For example, in an egalitarian society everyone may have very little wealth, whereas in the capitalist society some have vast amounts, some moderate amounts, and some very little. But some equality is worth sacrificing for increased wealth and freedom. Better that some have more than others, as long as everyone has enough, than that all have an equal amount (or an equally deserved amount) when it is minimal or insufficient for a good life. At this point utilitarians make an adjustment and, via the principle of *diminishing marginal utility*, advocate progressive income tax, redistributing some of the wealth from the very wealthy to the very poor. The principle of *diminishing marginal utility* holds that, all things being equal, a fixed amount of wealth will increase utility as it is transferred from the rich to the poor. Imagine three people, Sam, Susan, and Sally, who are hungry. Sam has seven pizzas while Susan and Sally have none. Sam is sated after two pizzas, so taking four pizzas from him and giving them to Susan and Sally, whose mouths are longingly watering for pizzas would maximize utility without harming Sam. So redistributing the surplus pizzas would maximize utility. Opponents to such redistribution object as follows: "Suppose that Sam has worked hard for those pizzas. Wouldn't it matter whether Susan and Sally had at least tried their best to find remunerative employment? If Susan did, but Sally didn't, we might prefer to satisfy Susan more than Sally. In addition, we might not want to take from Sam if by so doing we would dampen his incentive to work hard." The objection includes three important concepts, which we will discuss in this book: incentives, property, and desert. I will only offer a brief remark on each of them at this point. (1) Incentives are an important feature of morality and politics, for unless there is an incentive to work and to obey the law, for that matter, society will flounder. Incentive schemes are connected to utility, which, if carried out in a reasonable way, enhance the common good. If the free enterprise system provides the kind of incentive scheme that will best serve the common good, it should be supported. If it does not, it should be replaced by another institution. (2) Property rights are important for individual and social flourishing, as we will note in Chapter 3. But such rights are qualified and not absolute. We have a right to possess our bodies, minds, and material goods, but we are also stewards of these goods for the good of the society. (3) Desert is a vital moral and political concept, because it is inextricably tied up with responsibility without which we lose our human dignity and autonomy. So, as I will argue in the next chapter, it must play a significant role in any theory of political philosophy.

If we conjoin these three notions, we can give an initial response to the objector: Although a free-market economic system seems to work better than any competitor in producing aggregate wealth, some redistribution for the common good is justified. Progressive income tax in order to redistribute wealth from the rich to the deserving poor is based in part on this notion of diminishing marginal utility. Society aims at a threshold wherein people's basic needs of food and shelter may be met; so, while respecting essential property, it should take from the surplus of the rich in order to bring the poor up to a sustainable threshold.

Status Disequilibrium

It frequently happens that people with a lot of money have low social status or that people with high professional status are paid relatively low wages. A mafia boss has low social status but is probably financially affluent, whereas a teacher has fairly high social status but a meager salary. Teachers, especially university teachers, do not generally make as much money as businesspersons or engineers, but they obtain greater fulfillment that more than compensates for their modest wages. In the Middle Ages the notion of a just wage existed. Such a notion is absent from our conceptual scheme, inasmuch as market forces dictate what one is paid, but it may be that justice requires that we qualify market forces, supplementing salaries of socially admirable jobs like teachers with additional benefits depending on the resources available. We do tax the wealthy at higher rates than the poor. There is no reason we could not supplement the wages of the poor and the underpaid with tax revenues, paying teachers and nurses more nearly what they deserve. Perhaps those who have socially necessary but onerous jobs like garbage collectors and prison guards should (ideally) be paid more than professional entertainers and athletes. The principle would be: positions should be remunerated in inverse proportion to their inherent enjoyment or fulfillment. Those who bear greater, more onerous burdens should more nearly be compensated for their sacrifice. A system of economic justice would thereby supplement market capitalism. Some day we may discover a way to do this, but we are a long way from it now.

Conclusion

Although justice is not the only social and political virtue, it is one of the three most significant ones, along with liberty and utility. Every major political theory promotes both justice and liberty, though it combines them differently. Liberty, especially negative liberty, requires the noninterference by others, including the government, in the affairs of individuals, whereas distributive justice has to do with the distribution of benefits and burdens among people in a society. Utility is also an economic and social virtue. We seek the overall welfare and well-being of society. No one praises a society in which everyone is equally badly off because of a poor economy. Sometimes liberty or utility come into conflict with justice and at times may even override it. But, all things being equal, justice trumps other social virtues.

We will examine the various candidates for a theory of justice in the next three chapters. In Chapter 2 I will analyze the Classic Desert Theory, in Chapter 3, the Libertarian Theory, and in Chapter 4, the Welfare Liberal Theory of Justice. However, Michael Walzer, Nicholas Rescher, and others have argued that justice has a contextual dimension, rooted in the internal workings of cultural development. There seem to be several spheres of justice, each with its own internal logic. I will develop this pluralist aspect of justice in Chapter 5. In Chapter 6 I will examine the relationship of equality to justice, namely, equal opportunity. In Chapter 7 I will expand the theory of justice to include global concerns, dealing with cosmopolitan justice. In Chapter 8 I will examine retributive justice, including capital punishment.

Let us turn now to the Classic Theory of Justice.

Notes

1. This refers to distributive justice, which I mainly discuss in this chapter. Retributive justice, to be discussed in Chapter 8, has to do with punishment and needs a separate treatment.

2. William Paley, *Principles of Moral and Political Philosophy* (1785), III, pt I, ch I.

3. For a defense of the thesis of a universal set of moral norms , see, for example: David Brink, *Moral realism and the Foundations of Ethics* (NYC Cambridge University Press, 1989); John Finnis, *Moral Absolutes: Tradition, Revision and Truth* (Washington, DC: Catholic University of America Press, 1991); and Louis Pojman, *Ethics: Discovering Right and Wrong* (Belmont, CA: Wadsworth, 2002). For a defense of moral relativism, see J. L. Mackie, *Ethics: Inventing Right and Wrong* (New York: Penguin, 1976).

4. Kevin Bales, *Disposable People* (Berkeley: University of California Press, 2000), pp. 1–2. Seba eventually escaped to tell her story.

5. This is not to deny that people may be absolved of injustice through ignorance or that the principle may be overridden by other moral considerations, such as the survival of society.

6. Thomas Aquinas, *Basic Writings of Saint Thomas Aquinas*, vol. 2, Anton Pegis, ed. (New York: Random House, 1945), pp. 742ff.

7. Thomas Hobbes, *Leviathan* (1651), Ch. 13.

8. Joel Feinberg makes this point in *Social Philosophy* (Englewood Cliffs, NJ: Prentice Hall, 1973), pp. 100f.

9. W. Sadurski, *Giving Desert Its Due* (Dordrecht, Holland: Kluwer, 1986), pp. 15–21. Sadurski denies that the treatment of cruel punishment is an instance of noncomparative injustice, arguing that cruelty is morally wrong but not unjust. But on his own theory of desert, he is mistaken, for in cruel punishments, the criminal is made to bear a greater burden than he deserves.

10. Aristotle, *Nicomachean Ethics* (1137b).

11. I am indebted to Nicholas Rescher who makes this point and gives this example in *Fairness* (New Brunswick, NJ:Transaction Press, 2002), p. 29.

12. De Tocqueville, *Democracy in America* (New York: Doubleday, 1969), p. 57. See his indictment of America on this score on p. 41 of his book.

13. Some philosophers and economists, who believe that the free market will produce more wealth and should be left alone, reject the idea of social justice as a viable moral principle. The Nobel Prize winner, economist F. A. Hayek, writes:

> I may, as a result of long endeavors to trace the destructive effect which the invocation of 'social justice' has had on our moral sensitivity, and of again and again finding even eminent thinkers thoughtlessly using the phrase, have become unduly allergic to it, but I have come to feel strongly that the greatest service I can still render to my fellow men would be that I could make the speakers and writers among them thoroughly ashamed ever again to employ the term "social justice" (F. A. Hayek, *Law, Legislation and Liberty*).

CHAPTER 2

The Classical Theory of Justice as Desert

Aristotle: All men agree that what is just in distribution must be according to desert in some sense, though they do not all specify the same sort of desert, but democrats identify it with the status of freeman, supporters of oligarchy with wealth (or with noble birth), and supporters of aristocracy with excellence.

(Aristotle, *Nicomachean Ethics* Book V)

Justice is a constant and perpetual will to give every man his due. The principles of law are these: to live virtuously, not to harm others, to give his due to everyone. Jurisprudence is the knowledge of divine and human things, the science of the just and the unjust.

Law is the art of goodness and justice. By virtue of this [lawyers] may be called priests, for we cherish justice and profess knowledge of goodness and equity, separating right from wrong and legal from the illegal.[1]

(Ulpian)

The Classic Concept of Justice as Desert

This concept accords with our everyday speech. We say that the laborer deserves his wages, that as a person sows, so should he reap. We say, "one good deed deserves another," signifying that the principle of reciprocity is really one of responsibility for repaying favors. Most of us hold that equal work deserves equal pay, regardless of the race or gender of the worker. We ask, "Why do bad things happen to good people?" So we are distressed when an innocent child is sexually abused or a hard-working parent is struck down by a criminal's bullet. We are revolted when evil is returned for good, believing that the benefactor deserved better. We believe that the best qualified candidate deserves the job. We believe that the virtuous deserve to be happy and the evil people deserve to be punished and unhappy. We believe that criminals and traitors deserve censure and punishment for their heinous deeds, in proportion to the gravity of their crimes. Hence, Timothy McVeigh, the man responsible for the 1995 bombing of the Murrah Federal Building in Oklahoma City which killed 168 people, deserves severe punishment, possibly the death penalty, which he received. We say that the victims of the terrible terrorist attack on the World Trade Towers on September 11, 2001, didn't deserve such an evil attack and that their families deserve compensation from the sources that supported the al Qaeda terrorist network. We believe excellence deserves rewards. So we think that Barry Bonds deserved to win the American League Most Valuable Player Award for the sixth time in 2003, since his hitting record was phenomenal. We believe that heroes deserve rewards and cruel people deserve sanctions. Most people believe that someone who does not forgive others their failings does not deserve forgiveness for his or her failings. We think that injured parties sometimes deserve compensation for injuries done to them by physicians or businessmen through malpractice. Virtually every day we see examples of the important role desert plays in our lives.

The symbol of justice is a blindfolded woman, holding a pair of equally balanced scales in her hand, the metaphor pointing to the absolute symmetry between the quality of the human actions on the right side and the rewards or punishments on the left side. Justice is blind to irrelevant considerations (which birth, social status, race, and gender usually are), concerned only with giving one what he or she deserves. The earliest definition of justice in Western literature is found in Book I of Plato's *Republic*, "justice consists in rendering to each his due,"[2] in Aristotle's "distribution in proportion to merit" (*kat' axian*),[3] and the Roman equivalent *suum cuique tribuere* ("render to each his due"), as is reflected in Ulpian's *Corpus Juris*, quoted at the head of this chapter: "Justice is a constant and perpetual will to give every man his due," giving every person what he or she deserves, based on the person's character traits, including ability, virtues and vices. If you are excellent, you merit a suitable reward. If you are vicious, you deserve punishment; if mediocre, a mediocre benefit. Plato's Republic was a meritocracy, made up of people in three classes, according to their abilities. But the idea of desert, focusing more on moral actions than on talents, is found earlier than Plato or Ulpian in Eastern thought, in the doctrine of karma, which holds that there is a lawlike relationship between one's deeds and one's status in a future reincarnated life.

The three major Western religions hold to the thesis that justice consists of rendering to each what he or she deserves. On Judgment Day each one will be rewarded or punished according to his works, the good receiving rewards and the bad receiving punishments in proportion to the moral quality of their lives. Paul writes: "Whatsoever a man sows that shall he also reap" (Gal. 6:7). Kant was so impressed by the doctrine of justice as desert that he made it a premise in his argument for life after death. Justice, as a function of the moral law, requires that the righteous be recompensed with happiness in proportion to their virtue and the unrighteous be punished in proportion to their vice. This does not occur in this life, where the good often lose out and the bad often succeed. So there must be a life after death where justice occurs. While one may hesitate to endorse this argument, it is a testimony to our deep-seated intuition that justice consists in rendering to people according to their moral worth.[4]

Similar sentiments characterize specifically Christian statements about justice.[5] Writing from within the Christian tradition, G.W. Leibniz wrote:

Thus it is that the pains of the damned continue, even when they no longer serve to turn them away from evil, and that likewise the rewards of the blessed continue, even when they no longer serve for strengthening them in good. One may say nevertheless that the damned ever bring upon themselves new pains through new sins, and that the blessed ever bring upon themselves new joys by new progress in goodness: for both are founded on the principle of the fitness of things, which has seen to it that affairs were so ordered that the evil action must bring upon itself chastisement.[6]

Although most people find the idea of fittingness intuitively plausible, if not self-evident, the intuition can be traced back to our idea of responsibility. I will explain this later.

We get another hint of this *fittingness* or symmetry in the practice of gratitude. We normally and spontaneously feel grateful for services rendered. Someone treats us to dinner, gives us a present, teaches us a skill, rescues us from a potential disaster, or simply gives us directions. We normally feel spontaneous gratitude to our bene-factor. We want to reciprocate and benefit the bestower of blessing. On the other hand, if someone intentionally and cruelly hurts us, deceives us, or betrays our trust, we automatically feel resentment. We want to reciprocate and harm that person. Adam Smith and Henry Sidgwick argued that these basic emotions were in fact the grounds for our notion of desert: punishment was resentment universalized, and rewards—a sort of positive punishment—gratitude universalized.[7] Whether such a reduction of desert to resentment and gratitude completely explains our notion of desert may be questioned, but I for one do feel a universalized sense of resentful out-rage when I hear of criminals raping and murdering, and I feel something analogous to gratitude—call it "vicarious gratitude"—when I hear of works of charity, such as those of Mother Teresa. These reactive feelings may well be the natural origins of our sense of justice. They have a normative core: those whom I resent "ought" to suffer, and those towards whom I feel gratitude "ought" to prosper. Of course, my sentiments–judgments are not infallible and may not even be valid. But if we can link them with the nature of morality itself, with promoting or detracting from human flourishing, we can moralize the reactive attitudes.

This primordial desert-based idea of justice has two parts. Every action in the universe has a fitting response in terms of creating a duty to punish or reward, and that response must be *appropriate* in measure to the original action. It follows that evil deeds must be followed by evil outcomes and good deeds by good outcomes, exactly equal or in proportion to the vice or virtue in question. That is the basis of a primordial meritocracy, recognized in all cultures and major religions, though denied or undermined by much of contemporary political philosophy.

The eminent cultural anthropologist, George Casper Homans, observes: "Men are alike in holding the notion of proportionality between investment and profit that lies at the heart of distributive justice," and "Fair exchange, or distribu-tive justice in the relations among men, is realized when the profit, or reward less cost, of each man is directly proportional to his investment."[8]

Many people think that Karl Marx is an opponent of the classic notion of justice based on desert, since he famously uttered the formula for distributive justice, "From each according to his ability, to each according to his need." But this would be to misinterpret Marx, who actually defends the classic notion. In his *Critique of the Gotha Program*, Marx attacks utopian communists like LaSalle for uncritically adopting the needs-based motto. Distribution according to need should only take place in the ideal communist society, where everyone is equally deserving, since they are all contributing according to their maximal ability. Until that time, in the socialist society, the motto must be "from each according to his ability, to each according to his contribution."[9] Indeed, Marx's condemnation of capitalism is based on the classical idea of justice as desert. His Labor Theory of Value condemns capitalists as vampires and parasites for stealing and exploiting the workers. Say that a worker makes a chair with a certain labor value, deriving from his skill and labor, and we give it a value of 100, translating that into monetary terms, $100. The capitalist only pays the worker a fraction of his value, say $25, keeping the rest for himself, thus growing rich on such exploitative thefts. Of course, the capitalist has a right to deduct overhead costs from the total value, the costs of the raw material and machines used, say $10, but he goes far beyond that and robs the worker of the remainder, the other $65. This is unjust, claims Marx, for the worker deserves far more than he receives. Exploitation is giving people less than they deserve, less than you owe them.

My point, of course, is not to defend Marx's Labor Theory of Value but to indicate how widespread it is in the history of Western thought. It was held both by the father of capitalism, Adam Smith, as well as the greatest anticapitalist, Karl Marx; both by the greatest deontologist, Immanuel Kant, and by the greatest Utilitarian John Stuart Mill, who thought that rewarding people according to their deserts would lead to maximal utility. The Intuitionist W. D. Ross uses a thought experiment to establish the doctrine of justice as desert:

> If we compare two imaginary states of the universe, alike in the total amounts of virtue and vice and of pleasure and pain present in the two, but in one of which the virtuous were all happy and the vicious miserable, while in the other the virtuous were miserable and the vicious happy, very few people would hesitate to say that the first was a much better state of the universe than the second. It would seem then that, besides virtue and pleasure, we must recognize, as a third independent good, the apportionment of pleasure and pain to the virtuous and the vicious respectively. And it is on the recognition of this as a separate good that the recognition of the duty of justice, in distinction from fidelity to promise on the one hand and from beneficence on the other, rests.[10]

Such intuitions as these, that justice consists in receiving benefits and burdens in accordance with our deserts, seem to be rooted in our notion of responsibility. Being responsible entails being worthy of praise or blame and reward or punishment, depending on the quality of the act itself. The murderer, say a sniper who murders innocent people in cold blood, deserves punishment as a consequence of his deed, just as the moral saint, say Mother Teresa, deserves our gratitude and honor as a consequence of her deeds. That is, our actions have appropriate normative features attached to them. Some kinds of acts are inherently good or morally worthy and should be followed by good results in the agents. And some are inherently or morally evil and should be followed by harmful consequences in the agent. There is a secondary consequentialist argument for giving people what they deserve. Such a practice will provide an incentive for good actions and a deterrence for evil actions.

Primate studies suggest that a sense of justice as desert prevails even among monkeys. Capuchin monkeys were given tasks of bringing stones to their researchers. They were rewarded with cucumbers. That was fine, and all worked hard as long as everyone got the same reward for the same work. But when some monkeys were rewarded with grapes (a highly prized food) for the same work, the other monkeys slowed their output and some stopped working altogether, suggesting that a primitive sense of justice is inborn.[11] Children have similar reactions to unfairness.

Natural and Institutional Desert

It seems then that there are two basic types of desert: natural and institutional. *Natural desert* consists in treating people according to their effort or merit, rewarding or punishing them based on the intrinsic quality of their actions. So we naturally honor integrity, benevolence, and courage and seek to reward it, while we condemn laziness, cruelty, ingratitude, greed, and cowardice, even where no institutions exist. We think it is fitting that the industrious farmer profit from his hard work. If in the wilderness where no civilization or institutions exist a stranger saves my life, I ought to express gratitude for this benevolent act. On the other hand, much of our desert language is specific to institutions. We create games like baseball, football, and Olympic Games and then reward players and teams for their success. There are winners and losers within the game, determined by the rules of the games. Where there is no game, no one can deserve the prize for first place. Similarly, only when we have the institutions of medicine and law does it make sense to say that the best candidates should be admitted into medical school and law school. The law is a fundamental social institution that determines what constitutes deserving. Being vicious may deserve moral condemnation in the state of nature, but in civilized society we punish the act of violence with appropriate penalties, "letting the punishment fit the crime." The classic theory of justice differs from some modern theories like Rawls's theory of *justice as fairness* (see Chapter 4), which seems to hold that there is no pre-institutional (i.e., natural) desert. While many desert claims occur within an institutional framework, the classic theory of justice holds that cases of natural justice occur: the industrious deserve the fruits of their labor, courage and benevolence deserve admiration and reward, benefactors deserve gratitude, and cruelty and cowardice deserve our disapprobation.

Consider the Good Samaritan who discovered a wounded victim of a robber, probably a Jew, along the road. He binds the victim's wounds and takes him to an inn, where the wounded man receives medical attention, which the Samaritan pays for. Surely, this is the paradigm of moral goodness, yet no institutional arrangement existed requiring that Samaritans care for Jews, who despised Samaritans. Suppose now that the Good Samaritan returns the next day to visit the man.

Suppose the Jew now beats him, robs him of his money, and makes off with his donkey. Was not an injustice done? Even though no institutional arrangement existed between the Samaritan and the Jew, natural morality would inform us that the Jew acted unjustly.

One problem with the institutional view of desert is that it collapses the distinction between desert and entitlement. For example, many people believe that Al Gore deserved to win the 2000 presidential election, since he won the popular vote and the Florida count was in doubt, but on the basis of the Supreme Court decision, George Bush was entitled to the presidency. If one identifies all desert with institutional desert, one cannot make this distinction, nor can one argue that some institutions are unjust. Institutional desert entails moral relativism, so that if the institution of slavery exists, it is unjust to help liberate a slave. Most of us hold that slavery is naturally unjust. If we do, then a cogent case for some instances of natural desert can be made.

The Bases for Desert

Desert is a three-place relationship. The formula is:

S ought to receive some X by virtue of B

where S is the subject, X is the treatment (reward or punishment) and B is the basis (action or character trait) that justifies S receiving X.

For example, the convicted murderer ought to receive a harsh penalty for his crime, because he intentionally committed the murder. Similarly, we might say that the doctor ought to receive our gratitude for saving our mother's life.

Joel Feinberg has given the contemporary classic analysis of desert as a preinstitutional or natural concept.[12] He argues that desert is a heterogeneous notion, having at least five main classes: (1) awards and prizes; (2) assignments of grades; (3) rewards and punishments; (4) praise, blame, and other informal responses (e.g., applause); and (5) reparations, liability, and modes of compensation. Notably absent from his list is the economic application of desert, which comes into play only as compensation for hazardous work. Because desert is a heterogeneous or pluralist notion, different qualities will serve as fitting bases for desert attribution in different contexts. The basis for awarding first prize in a race will be covering the required distance in the shortest time. The basis of receiving a grade in school is the quality of the performance. The basis for deserving punishment is the committing of a crime. Among standard candidates for deservingness are effort, need, merit, equality, contribution, and moral virtue. It is a subject of considerable debate as to which of these candidates are legitimate bases of desert. How do we decide which criteria to accept? Some philosophers hold that *responsibility* is a necessary and core condition for being deserving:

S deserves X only if S is responsible for Y, the desert base of X.

This seems plausible at first glance. The criminal only deserves to be punished for a crime for which he is responsible, and the inventor only deserves a reward for his invention if he is responsible for it. As we noted earlier, our notion of responsibility entails the concept of desert, but desert may not always entail the concept of responsibility. The formula that desert entails responsibility holds for the quality of effort, but it fails to cover compensatory desert. We normally say that the victims of a crime or malpractice deserve compensation even though no effort on their part is relevant to their case. The innocent victims of the Enron Corporation scandal, the thousands of workers who lost their pensions, deserve financial compensation from the executives of the corporation who were culpable for their loss. It seems that compensation is an exception to the responsibility thesis. Perhaps we can say someone is responsible in the compensation case, but it is the violator of one's right, not the victim. The victim deserves compensation by virtue of someone being responsible for his or her harm. But some philosophers argue that no one needs to be responsible for the harm for the victim to be deserving. If a child contracts polio or blindness or some other disease through no fault of anyone, he or she deserves compensation for this disability.[13] Other philosophers hold that compensatory desert requires an agent to be responsible for the harm, and since nature is not an agent, no injustice is involved. Not all evil is the result of human agency.

The idea of responsibility as a criterion for distributing goods seems to rule out need as a desert base, since one can be needy because of negligence or one's own bad choices. We should help the needy out of benevolence, but not out of justice, unless we are responsible for their plight. The idea of desert seems to rule out equality as a desert base, since some people may be more deserving then others by virtue of their actions or contribution. However, some philosophers like Kant hold a theory of equal human worth which would entail equal respect for each human being. That is, each person deserves to be treated with dignity, as an end in him or herself, not as a mere means. Kant, however, thought that equality was only the starting point and that one could forfeit one's dignity through immoral behavior. As we noted earlier, he held to a classic desert theory of justice. The classic theory of justice focusing on appraising attitudes centers on effort and merit as the standard desert bases. We now turn to the concept of merit and desert.

Merit and Desert

Let us continue our examination of the desert theory by distinguishing between two related concepts: desert and merit, which, as is the case with Feinberg, are often used as synonyms. Although both are appraisal terms and ordinary language uses them in multifaceted and overlapping ways, sometimes they have different central meanings. From an analytic perspective, merit seems a broader concept, the genus of which desert is the species. Merit, corresponding to the Greek word *axia*, is any feature or quality that is the basis for distributing positive (or in the case of demerit, negative) attribution, such as praise, rewards, prizes (or penalties and punishments), and grades. We find the concept in Homer's writings, as is argued by A.W.H. Adkins:

> The Homeric king does not gain his position on the grounds of strength and fighting ability. He belongs to a royal house, and inherits wealth, derived from the favored treatment given to his ancestors, which provides full armor, a chariot, and leisure. Thus equipped, he and his fellow agathoi [nobles], who are similarly endowed, form the most efficient force for attack and defence which Homeric society possesses. Should they be successful, their followers have every reason to commend them as agathoi and their way of life as arete [virtuous]; should they fail, their followers have every reason to regard this failure, voluntary or not, as aischron [shameful]. A failure . . . in the Homeric world must result either in slavery or annihilation. Success is so imperative that only results have any value; intentions are unimportant.[14]

Merit signifies an appraising attitude (positive or negative), such as gratitude, praise, approval, and admiration. Nondeserved merit can consist in features which the Natural Lottery has distributed, such as your basic intelligence, personality type, skin color, good looks, Irish smiling eyes, good upbringing, noble heritage, and genetic endowments. In Homeric society, it denoted nobility who could protect the state: For us it connotes any one of a plurality of traits from high intelligence to attractiveness or athletic ability. But it may be appraisal specific, depending on the context. The most beautiful dog in the canine beauty contest merits the first prize, the tallest person in the city merits the prize for being the tallest person in the city, and an Asian detective may merit the high-paying job of being a spy in an Asian neighborhood harassed by Chinese criminals because race is a relevant characteristic for that position, even though he did nothing to deserve his Asian ancestry. In these situations beauty, tallness, and being Asian become meritorious traits, whereas ugliness, shortness, and whiteness are demerits. The formula for merit is:

S merits M in virtue of some characteristic (or quality) Q which S possesses

where S is the subject, M is the thing that S ought to receive, and Q is the merit base, the good (or bad) quality possessed by S.

Desert, on the other hand, is typically or paradigmatically connected with action, since it rests on what we voluntarily do or produce. It is typically connected with intention or effort. As George Sher writes:

> Of all the bases of desert, perhaps the most familiar and compelling is diligent, sustained effort. Whatever else we think, most of us agree that persons deserve things for sheer hard work. We believe that conscientious students deserve to get good grades, that athletes who practice regularly deserve to do well, and that businessmen who work long hours deserve to make money. Moreover, we warm to the success of immigrants and underprivileged who

have overcome obstacles of displacement and poverty. Such persons, we feel, richly deserve any success they may obtain.[15]

I deserve to win the race because I have trained harder than anyone else. You deserve praise for your kind act because it was a product of a morally good will. The man or woman who works hard at a socially useful job deserves more in terms of salary than the person who loafs or works half-heartedly. The Good Samaritan deserved gratitude for helping the helpless, wounded man who was mugged on his way to Jericho. His deed deserved to be reciprocated preinstitutionally, but he would have deserved praise even if his efforts failed. On the other hand, your native intelligence, reflected in a high IQ, may be merited but not deserved, since you were born with it and didn't do anything to deserve it; a prize for being the youngest person in the room is merited but not deserved, since there's nothing the person did to deserve it; and receiving an A on a test over material you effortlessly mastered was something you merited more than you deserved. Similarly, a black actor's claim on the part of playing Othello in Shakespeare's play has merit, although the actor did nothing to deserve his skin color.

Some philosophers doubt that the merit/desert distinction is very strong. But consider: Suppose in times gone by a subspecies of humans was created through genetic manipulation with wings and light bodies, so that they could fly. Such people had great social utility, for they could fly over mountains or enemy lines with important goods or information. When there was need of a secure messenger, they would typically get picked over more earth-bound mortals. The flyers obtained higher salaries than walkers and enjoyed great fame and social prestige—much as star athletes do today.

The flyers didn't deserve their wings, but they certainly merited the employment and honors they were given. They were the best candidates for flying to distant places—and reaching their destinations safely and securely. Were there no need of rapid, distant communication, their wings would have had only aesthetic value. The need for a means of communicating over long distances created the institutional value of rewarding winged people.

Contrast this with the person who does everything he can to live a virtuous life, to practice benevolence and contribute to the social good. This person deserves praise and honor in a way the flyer may not. (Let us suppose that the flyer flies almost effortlessly.) One merits goods, whereas the second person deserves them.

John Stuart Mill contrasts these two criteria of justice when he asks by which criterion workers should be rewarded—according to desert (effort) or merit (efficiency and productivity):

> In a co-operative industrial association, is it just or not that talent or skill should give a title to superior remuneration? On the negative side of the question it is argued, that whoever does the best he can, deserves equally well, and ought not in justice to be put in a position of inferiority for no fault of his own; that superior abilities have already advantages more than enough, in the admiration they excite, the personal influence they command, and the internal

sources of satisfaction attending them, without adding to these a superior share of the world's goods; and that society is bound in justice rather to make compensation to the less favored, for this unmerited inequality of advantages, than to aggravate it.

On the contrary side it is contended, that society receives more from the more efficient laborer; that his services being more useful, society owes him a larger return for them; that a greater share of the joint result is actually his work, and not to allow his claim to it is a kind of robbery; that if he is only to receive as much as others, he can only be justly required to produce as much, and to give a smaller amount of time and exertion, proportioned to his superior efficiency.[16]

In this appeal to conflicting principles, justice has two sides: "the one looks to what it is just that the individual should receive, the other to what it is just that the community should give."

As we noted, Feinberg calls such meritorious qualities as intelligence, native athletic ability, good upbringing "the bases of desert," meaning that while we may not deserve these traits, they can generate desert claims. That is, while you may not deserve your superior intelligence or tendency to work hard, you do deserve the high grade on your essay that is a joint product of your intelligence and effort.

The formula for desert is:

S deserves D in virtue of doing (or attempting to do) A

where S is a subject, D is the property, thing, or treatment deserved, and A is the act, the desert base for D.

Desert, then, is closely connected to effort and intention, whereas merit signifies positive qualities that call forth a positive response. Whereas God, knowing our inner motivations, rewards purely on the basis of desert, we fallible beings, being far less certain as to how to measure effort and intentionality, tend to reward merit, the actual contribution or positive results produced. You and I may both get the same merit pay bonus for producing 100 more widgets than the average worker, but I may deserve them more than you do, since your superior native ability enabled you to produce them effortlessly, whereas I had to strain every ounce of strength to get the same result.

We can further divide desert into moral and nonmoral desert. Moral desert corresponds to the Kantian good will, the intention to do one's duty or go beyond what duty requires. The moral person deserves happiness in proportion to the degree of his good will. Nonmoral desert has to do with effort in morally acceptable activities. Of two people of equal ability, the one who trains more diligently and exerts himself more (nonmorally) deserves to win in the competition, even if by bad luck (e.g., he accidentally trips), the less deserving runner actually wins. We should qualify "nonmoral desert" with the phrase "morally acceptable activities," since we would not say that the thief who trains hard to burgle deserves to be successful or the maniac who becomes skilled in assassination deserves to succeed in assassinating the president. Wittgenstein gives an example in another connection which nicely illustrates the difference. Suppose, while playing a game of tennis, someone reprimands me, "You ought to work harder to play a better game." I might reply, "I don't want to—it's not that important," without receiving serious censure. But if, on failing to do my moral duty, someone said to me, "You ought to work harder to be a conscientious person," and I replied, "I don't want to—it's not that important," I would rightly be censured. There is a difference in moral and nonmoral obligations. No one can reasonably censure the mediocre tennis player for not improving, but we can reprove those who do not strive for moral excellence.

An interesting example of the conflict between desert and merit occurred during the Olympic Games in Atlanta, Georgia (August 3, 1996). Carl Lewis, one of the leading United States' athletes, having won his ninth gold medal in the long jump, requested that he be added to the United States' men's 400 meter relay team. He argued that, because of his superior ability, he merited it. Many athletes and fans agreed with him and requested that the coach substitute Lewis for one of the other runners. Some of the other spectators and runners, including those who feared being displaced by Lewis, were outraged at his audacity. They argued that Lewis shouldn't be put on the team because he didn't deserve to be on it in spite of his great talent, for he turned down the opportunity to enter the tryouts for the team. Those who made the team played by the rules, won their places in fair competition, and could legitimately expect to run. Here is a case where merit and desert seem to conflict, and where desert, it seems to me, wins out over merit. It wins out because we have a legitimate institution (the process of competing for a position on a team) in which those who play by the rules deserve to be rewarded with the positions that they fairly won.

The distinction between desert and merit as appraisal attitudes may be transformed into standard desert language by speaking of effort and merit or efficiency as two competing, but valid, desert-bases.

Finally, we may distinguish desert and merit from entitlement, positive rights. Even though I am a lazy bum who is undeserving of any wealth, I am entitled to the inheritance that my rich uncle bequeaths to me. For Rawls, as we will see in Chapter 4, all desert claims reduce to entitlements, and justified entitlements are those obtaining in a society governed by the principles of justice-as-fairness. But desert and merit seem more fundamental qualities than rights, which are primarily products of human institutions. The desert theory is really a two-pronged theory, stating that goods should be distributed on the basis of desert or merit, depending on the situation.

The Symmetry Argument

The classical theory of justice as desert consists in giving people what they deserve. Now we need to describe the symmetrical relationship between positive and negative desert.

A symmetrical relationship exists between positive and negative desert. The most basic form of positive desert is praising, and the most basic negative form is blaming. We praise people for what we perceive to be their good deeds, and we blame them for their bad deeds. We praise Sarah for giving hours of time to tutoring poor children or for feeding the indigent. We blame Sam for shirking his responsibility to provide for his children when he gambled away his week's earnings at the local casino. Rewards and punishments are extensions of this basic desert behavior. When the activity reaches a threshold of social seriousness, we not only praise or blame the behavior, but we also reward and punish it. When Sarah's aid to the poor is perceived to be of sufficient worth, we may grant her special recognition as Citizen of the Year. When a soldier engages in heroic action, we grant him a medal of honor. Conversely, when Sam commits a crime, we do not simply blame him, but we try him as a criminal and, if he is found guilty, we sentence him to an appropriate punishment.

We may call this symmetry relationship the *karmic principle* (in line with the Hindu-Buddhist principle that instructs us that as we sow, so shall we reap—except my principle is completely secular and based on morality, not religion or an afterlife).[17] Ideally, the virtuous should be happy in proportion to their virtuousness, and the evil should be unhappy in proportion to their viciousness.

Although the karmic principle is held as an ideal, we acknowledge our fallibility by being more circumspect in applying negative than positive desert. It is worse to mistakenly punish someone for an alleged crime than to mistakenly reward him for an alleged good deed. We commit a greater injustice in infringing on the liberty of a person in punishing him or her than we do in rewarding someone. We acknowledge this in the maxim that it is better to let 10 guilty men go free than to punish one innocent man. (Actually, this maxim is an exaggeration, but the point is well made that it is a tragedy to punish the innocent for a crime that the person has not committed.) So we presume the accused to be innocent until proven guilty. And the greater the crime involved, the greater the need for fairness and compelling evidence in order to overturn the presumption of innocence. On the other hand, we do not normally require the same level of scrutiny in rewarding people for their good deeds.

In both rewarding and punishing on the basis of desert, intention is a necessary condition for the attribution of the desert, though it is of more importance regarding punishment. If Sam accidentally or unintentionally discovers the cure for cancer or a kidnapped child, it is of no great moment if we reward him for his luck, but if Sid didn't intentionally kill Sarah, but only accidentally caused her death, we alter the charge from first degree murder to involuntary manslaughter, a charge warranting a lesser punishment than murder. Similarly, if we find that the accused is severely retarded or brain damaged, so that he didn't know what he was doing, we are likely to drop the charge of guilty but less likely to withdraw the reward.

We can represent our thesis in the form of a chart:

Positive	Negative
Approval	Disapproval
Praise	Blame
Reward	Punishment

Our actual practices of rewarding and punishing also have the secondary consequentialist purposes of encouraging good behavior and discouraging bad behavior. With this in mind, the Symmetry Principle can be expressed in two propositions R and P:

> R: We should *reward* person S for good act A because S deserves the reward on the basis of A, and, secondarily, rewarding S for A will encourage others to do A-type acts.

> P: We should *punish* person S for bad act B because S deserves the punishment on the basis of B, and, secondarily, punishing S for A will discourage others from doing B-type acts.

Our theory of desert is primarily retributive, but there is a connection between desert and secondary utilitarian goals.

One important consequence of this theory is to rule out other candidates as criteria for justice. Some philosophers hold that everyone should receive equal amounts of the society's resources. If the symmetry principle is correct, this is not so, since some people may not deserve benefits or punishments. Similarly, some philosophers hold that social goods ought to be distributed according to need. But this criterion fails to fit our theory. We would not punish someone, saying that he needed to be punished, nor would we reward someone on the basis of need. Someone may have a need for $1,000 but may not deserve it. It seems more accurate to say that our duty of meeting need is a function of benevolence (or mercy) rather than justice. Furthermore needs fluctuate according to economic and social conditions, whereas morality is universal and objective.

Objections to Desert-Based Justice

This is the classic doctrine of justice as desert, and today it is under siege. The leading political philosophers, from liberals like John Rawls and Stuart Hampshire to libertarians like F. A. Hayek and Robert Nozick, to communitarians like Michael Sandel, reject it. How did this come about? Philosophers have found three significant problems with the doctrine of desert which have led many to abandon it and others to subordinate it under other ideals. They are (1) a Criterion Problem, that is, determining exactly what is the appropriate desert base, contribution, performance, effort, or compensation; (2) the Epistemological Problem of measuring how much a person deserves; and (3) the Metaphysical Problem of determining whether the concept even is coherent. I will briefly examine each of these problems. We will examine a fourth criticism, the holistic objection, which is leveled against the symmetry aspect of the desert theory, when we examine the liberal theory of justice in Chapter 4.

1. *The Criterion Problem.* Should the relevant desert base be one's contribution, compensation, or effort? Take a simple example of the cooperative venture of three people pushing a car up a steep hill. Three people are pushing the car. A is

putting in the greatest effort, but B is the most effective, since he is the strongest, while C has made the greatest sacrifice to push the car, leaving his lucrative job for the afternoon in order to help out. How do we determine the relative values of these kinds of acts? Sometimes particular desert bases seem intuitively fitting, such as giving grades on the basis of performance rather than compensation or effort. The person who meets the highest standards receives the highest grade whether or not he or she made a great effort. Sometimes this problem can be solved, but at other times, it's not clear how to compare or apply desert bases. Since a case for the heterogeneity of desert bases seems cogent, one must admit that the competing criteria of desert are sometimes hard to adjudicate. In these cases a community is free to decide the matter by consensus or a vote.

2. *The Epistemological Problem.* An epistemological concern arises because of the increasing cooperative venture involved in modern labor. Desert seems more suitable to an agrarian world where each person is responsible for his own plot of land ("Whatsoever a man soweth that shall he also reap.") than to the complexities of modern industry. Even Marx's Labor Theory of Value seems misplaced, for few tables or chairs are made by single carpenters working alone. More typically, workers labor in cooperation with each other, so that it is a herculean task to measure the effort or contribution of any single individual. A hundred or more people may work on various aspects of materials in producing a final product, such as an automobile, airplane, ship, or skyscraper. How would one go about measuring who deserved what economic reward in producing an automobile's various components, let alone designed them and the car itself? It would be almost as difficult to measure the contribution of each member of both teams in a tug of war. As Rawls notes, even if we could figure out the ways to do the measuring, such measuring seems impracticable. This seems a valid objection. We cannot always know exactly how much a person deserves, but given the contextualized application of desert claims, we can divide and conquer. We will use different criteria in criminal cases than in grading math exams and awarding prizes for winning track and field events. We can normally rely on common sense to inform us whether someone intended to do a good or bad deed, and so deserve praise or blame.

3. *The Metaphysical Problem.* The metaphysical problem consists in determining whether the concept of desert is even coherent. Many philosophers have adopted a naturalist interpretation of human agency, which sees our actions based in a deterministic scheme, caused by factors over which we have no control, our genetic endowment and environment. Rawls put it like this:

> No one deserves his greater natural capacity nor merits a more favorable starting place in society. But it does not follow that one should eliminate these distinctions. There is another way to deal with them. The basic structure can be arranged so that these contingencies work for the good of the least fortunate. . . .
>
> It seems to be one of the fixed points of our considered judgments that no one deserves his place in the distribution of native endowments, any more than one deserves one's initial starting place in society. The assertion that a man

deserves the superior character that enables him to make the effort to cultivate his abilities is equally problematic; for his character depends in large part upon fortunate family and social circumstances for which he can claim no credit. The notion of desert seems not to apply to these cases. Thus the more advantaged representative man cannot say that he deserves and therefore has a right to a scheme of cooperation in which he is permitted to acquire benefits in ways that do not contribute to the welfare of others (*Theory of Justice*, p. 104).

The British philosopher Stuart Hampshire is even more explicit about the incoherence of desert:

> Is there anything whatever that, strictly speaking, a man can take credit for, or he can properly be said to deserve, with the implication that it can be attributed to him, the ultimate subject, as contrasted with the natural forces that formed him? In the last analysis, are not all advantages and disadvantages distributed by natural causes, even when they are the effects of human agency? . . . I think it would be better to think of all advantages, whether naturally acquired or conferred by men, as unearned and undeserved. . . . After genetic roulette and the roulette of childhood environment, a man emerges, so equipped, into the poker game of social competition, within a social system determined by largely unknown historical forces.[18]

The anti-desert argument runs like this.

1. If we deserve anything, we must be the authors of our own selves (in order to have the kind of free will necessary to be responsible for our actions and achievements).
2. We are not the authors of our own selves;
3. So we do not deserve anything.

It is true that we do not deserve our genetic endowment or the early environment we inherited. But couldn't we still be said to deserve what we make of those lottery-endowed traits? No, for even the tendency to make an effort is a product of deterministic, antecedent causes.

This anti-desert argument has persuaded a number of philosophers to reject the notion of desert, but is this a sound argument? I don't think it is. There are a number of places to attack it, but one quick way to defeat it is to present an argument for some kind of suitable free will, either the libertarian variety, which holds that some acts are caused by the self alone, rather than antecedent factors, or the compatibilist variety, which holds that as long as we act voluntarily (i.e., are not coerced by internal or external forces against our will), we are responsible for our actions, and so deserve what we get as a result. The arguments are complicated, so that I cannot develop them here, but anyone who thinks freedom of the will is true, will have reason to reject the Rawls–Hampshire argument.[19] Suffice it to say, not only does their argument defeat any notion of desert. It also destroys the notion of responsibility. If the argument against desert is sound, not only don't we deserve anything, but we are not responsible for anything either. Human responsibility is an illusion. For if everything is the product of the genetic-environmental lotteries, the serial roulette wheels of fortune, how can we be held responsible for our actions, good or bad? Hitler and his Nazi henchmen were not responsible for starting the Second World War or exterminating 6 million Jews; the Lotteries of Life were. Timothy McVeigh wasn't responsible for blowing up the Federal Building in Oklahoma City in 1996, the Roulette Wheels of destiny were. So why did we execute McVeigh in June 2001? Is it all a matter of bad luck and lotteries? But if we hold that moral responsibility is applicable to some of our acts, we will have ample grounds to hold to the doctrine of justice being the distribution of benefits and burdens according to what they deserve.

One further point should be made here. Although we do not deserve our natural talents, they define who we are. They along with our bodies and brains, which we do not deserve, are our essential property. We own them, so that no one has a right to infringe upon them. As long as we are not using them immorally or are using them to infringe upon the rights of others, we may use them to improve our lives.

Although Rawls makes use of the Natural Lottery Argument, he seems to place more weight on the impracticality (the epistemological problem) of making desert judgments. We must leave the discussion there for the moment and turn to the two accounts of the two criteria that have replaced desert as the material criterion of justice: *rights* and *need*. Rights, especially property rights, have been put forth by classical liberalism, sometimes known as libertarianism, as the content of justice. Need has been put forth as the criterion of justice by socialists and modern welfare liberals. In Chapter 3 we turn first to classical liberalism and the justification of property, beginning with the work of John Locke, and then with his most articulate twentieth-century disciple, Harvard philosopher Robert Nozick. Subsequently, in Chapter 4, we will examine the welfare liberalism of Nozick's teacher, the most important political philosopher of the twentieth century, John Rawls. In Chapter 5 we consider the pluralist theory of justice.

Conclusion

Justice as desert, which has been the classic notion of justice, accords with our reflective intuitions. Furthermore, it seems entailed by our concept of responsibility, for to be responsible means to be praiseworthy if you perform a task adequately, and blameworthy if you don't. That is, you deserve praise or blame depending on how you perform your task. The Desert Theory also has the advantage of symmetrically applying to both distributive and retributive conceptions of justice, including compensatory justice. Indeed, as primate studies demonstrate, we may be hard-wired as evolved animals to take desert as a foundation of distribution of rewards and punishment. Justice as Desert is at least a significant part of what justice consists in. It consists of a deserving (effort) aspect and merit (talent). In this manner it is complex. Whether it is the most satisfactory theory of justice remains to be seen. Let us begin to examine the main contemporary theories of justice.

Notes

1. Ulpian in the *Digest* of the Roman book of law *Corpus Juris*. Ca. A.D. 200.

2. *"ta opheilomena hekastoi apodidonai dikaion esti."*

3. *Nicomachean Ethics* 1131a. "All are agreed that justice in distributions must be based on Merit of some sort, although they do not all mean the same sort of merit *(axian)*. *Axia* is often translated "desert," but "merit" or "worth" is more accurate.

4. Immanuel Kant, *Critique of Practical Reason* (first published in 1788), translated by Lewis White Beck (Indianapolis: Bobbs-Merrill, 1956).

5. See Gal. 6:7, I Cor. 3:10-15; Heb. 6:2 and 9:7 and James 2:13f.

6. Leibniz, *Theodicy* (trans. E. M. Huggard), 1698.

7. Henry Sidgwick, *The Methods of Ethics* (Indianapolis, IN: Hackett Publishing Co, 1981), Book III, Ch 5.

8. George Caspar Homans, *Social Behavior: Its Elementary Forms* (Routledge & Kegan Paul, 1961), pp. 246, 264.

9. Karl Marx, *Critique of the Gotha Program*, published in *Karl Marx: Selected Writings*, ed. D. McLellan (Oxford: Oxford University Press, 1977), pp. 566f.

10. W. D. Ross, *The Right and the Good* (Oxford: Oxford University Press, 1930), p. 138.

11. Science/*Daily* Magazine www.sciencedaily.com. releases/ 2003/09/03.

12. Joel Feinberg, "Justice and Personal Desert" *Nomos VI: Justice*, eds. C. J. Friedrich and John Chapman (NY: Atherton, 1963).

13. Fred Feldman, "Desert: Reconsideration of Some Received Wisdom," *Mind* 104 (1995): 63–77.

14. A.W.H. Adkins, *Merit and Responsibility: A Study of Greek Values* (Oxford: Oxford University Press 1960), p. 35.

15. George Sher, *Desert* (Princeton, NJ: Princeton University Press, 1986), p. 53.

16. John Stuart Mill, Utilitarianism, ed. G. Sher (Indianapolis: Hackett, 1979), pp. 56–57 *(italics mine)*. Mill himself thought utility was the criterion by which to adjudicate the matter.

17. Analogues to the karmic principle are found in the Hebrew Bible (Ps 1) and the New Testament (Gal. 6:8 "Whatsoever a man sow that shall he also reap"). George Homans argues that virtually every culture examined by anthropologists includes such a principle [*Social Behavior* (NYC: Harcourt Brace, 1974)].

18. Stuart Hampshire, "Review of Rawls" *Theory of Justice in New York Review of Books*, 18:3 (February 24, 1972), pp. 34–39.

19. I have defended this strategy in my essay "Free Will, Determinism and Moral Responsibility : A Response to Galen Strawson" in my book *Ethical Theory*, 4th ed. (Belmont, CA: Wadsworth Publishing Co., 2002).

CHAPTER 3

The Libertarian Theory of Justice:
Robert Nozick

> It is very clear, that God, as King David says, Psalm. 115:16, "has given the earth
> to the children of men," given it to mankind in common. . . . Though the earth,
> and all inferior creatures, be common to all men, yet every man has a property in
> his own person: this no body has any right to but himself. The labor of his body,
> and the work of his hands, we may say, are properly his. Whatsoever then he
> removes out of the state that nature hath provided, and left it in, he hath mixed
> his labor with, and joined to it something that is his own, and thereby makes it
> his property. It being by him removed from the common state nature hath placed
> it in, it hath by this labor something annexed to it, that excludes the common
> right of other men. For this labor being the unquestionable property of the laborer,
> no man but he can have a right to what that is once joined to, at least where
> there is enough, and as good, left in common for others.
>
> (John Locke, *Second Treatise of Government*, 1789, Section 27)

Classical Liberalism and Justice: Rights
and the Justification of Property

Justice, according to John Rawls, is the dominant concept of economically
advanced societies like ours where contract and private property are key characteristics. Justice is not a dominant concept in primitive societies, where duties of
generosity and reciprocity reign. In many cultures, taking your neighbor's boat or
weapon when you need it is not considered stealing, since the idea of property is
not well defined. Societies concerned with social justice are generally relatively
stable, economically advanced communities, where private property is a dominant
institution. In primitive societies, the concept of justice is related more closely to
partiality and relationships than it is in our more impersonal society. For example,
in a primitive society it would be wrong not to give an important job to a close
relative, if one were a candidate, whereas in ours one would be charged with the
crime of nepotism.

All wealth is property, a word that comes from the Latin *proprietas*, meaning
ownership. All property was once unowned, as part of nature. This book is made
up of paper that comes from wood which comes from trees, having an ancient

pedigree in primeval forests that go back in time, before human beings. The bricks, stone, and steel of our buildings, molded and transformed by human labor, was once part of rock formations and sand deposits on glacial plains. Similarly, the grapes from which we ferment wine and the grains from which we make our bread appeared in nature long before humanity. If the Earth belongs to no man, how can human beings claim parts of it as their own? How does natural material become owned by individual people?

John Locke's justification of property in Chapter 5 of his *Second Treatise of Government* (henceforth, *Treatise*) offers the classical account of the origination and legitimacy of property. He writes the words quoted at the beginning of this section, that God has given the Earth to all men in common, but for our individual survival and enjoyment has allowed us to have our own property from which we can exclude others. "Whatsoever then he removes out of the state that nature hath provided, and left it in, he hath mixed his labor with, and joined to it something that is his own, and thereby makes it his property."

Originally, all things were owned in common, which meant that they were not really owned, in the sense that we could do whatever we wanted with the Earth's resources. But human beings had to eat or perish. They partook of the fruits and nuts of the forest in order to survive. If no one ever expropriated anything, all would die. Property acquisition is need-based. A person may take what he or she needs to survive. Locke, as a Christian, believed that God gave the Earth to humanity to use for their survival and enjoyment. We may take what we need and by mixing our labor with it make it our own. But God put two provisos on our use of nature:

> For this labor being the unquestionable property of the laborer, no man but he can have a right to what that is once joined to, at least where there is enough, and as good, left in common for others.
>
> Nor was this appropriation of any parcel of land, by improving it, any prejudice to any other man, since there was still enough, and as good left; and more than the yet unprovided could use. So that, in effect, there was never the less left for others because of his enclosure for himself. For he that leaves as much as another can make use of, does as good as take nothing at all. Nobody could think himself injured by the drinking of another man, though he took a good draught, who had a whole river of the same water left him to quench his thirst: And the case of land and water, where there is enough of both, is perfectly the same. (*Treatise*, Sect. 33)

The two provisos that must qualify each acquisition are: first, we must leave "enough, and as good" for others. That is, we must not hoard or greedily exclude others from the Earth's bounty. And, second, we must not waste. We must not take more than we need for our survival and flourishing. We have a right to property, extending from our own bodies to what we appropriate in nature and mix our labor with. But we are to be good stewards of the Earth, not abusing it or selfishly accumulating material possessions. The basic argument goes as follows:

1. I own my body and my labor. (They are my primary property.)
2. In laboring with nature, I mix my labor with the object.
3. Hence, if the object is unowned, it becomes my property.

The idea is that by changing part of nature through my work, say by turning a tree into a table or chair, I extend my body into the object. Is this true? We might point out that those who are not able to work cannot own anything in this primary way. In addition, the argument relies on a biblical account of human origins. If there is no God, it may not seem as cogent. In *Anarchy, State and Utopia* (*ASU*), Robert Nozick has pointed to a problem. The argument that mixing labor with nature or land entitles you to it seems to rely on a missing premise (P):

(P) If I own something and mix it with something else, that is unowned, I acquire ownership of that other thing. "Ownership seeps over into the rest."[1]

But why, Nozick asks, "isn't mixing what I own with what I don't own a way of losing what I own rather than a way of gaining what I don't? If I own a can of tomato juice and spill it into the sea so that its molecules (made radioactive, so I can check this) mingle evenly throughout the sea, do I thereby come to own the sea, or have I foolishly dissipated my tomato juice?" (*ASU*, p. 175) But, humorous as the counterexample is, it seems uncharitable to Locke. For dumping the can of tomato juice into the sea would not be directly mixing your labor with the sea, and presuming to gain possession of the sea in this way would violate the proviso of leaving as good and as much for others. It would be a greedy self-aggrandizement. As Nozick himself points out, it would not add value to the sea. Locke has in mind such activities as cutting down unowned trees and using the wood to build your house and fences, cultivating the land, planting corn and potatoes. Here the argument takes on an aspect of desert, "what a man sows that should he reap." By expending energy and intelligent effort he transforms a part of the forest into a farm. The laborer deserves the fruits of his labor, whereas the freeloader who takes the farmer's goods deserves nothing.

Once the property is yours you may sell it or give it away, but you may not destroy it wantonly, since you are a steward of property that ultimately belongs to God. There is still the problem of inheritance. If the only reason you have a lot of property and I very little is because your great, great grandfather came here before my father, this seems unfair. At any rate, Locke's argument seems more applicable to a pioneer society, like settlers in America's Western frontier, but seems less applicable in most countries today where virtually all the inhabitable land is already owned. There simply isn't "enough, and as good" left over for others.

We can understand why Rousseau would rail against the notion of private property:

> The first man who, having enclosed a piece of ground, bethought of saying, "This is mine," and found people simple enough to believe him, was the true founder of civil society. For how many crimes, wars, murders, from how many horrors and misfortunes might not any one have saved mankind by pulling up the stakes or filling up the ditches and crying to his fellows, "Do not listen to this impostor. You will be ruined if you forget that the fruits of the earth belong to us all, and the earth itself belongs to no one."[2]

Private property in a world of scarcity and need can be challenged. P. J. Proudhon said "Property is theft" and Marxists would abolish private property. On the other hand, Hume argued that private property has great utility. It provides security and enjoyment that enhance our lives. Even if one does not completely accept Locke's argument, one might be persuaded by Hume's common-sense utilitarian reasoning. Even communist countries permit people to own their own private goods, such as owning one's car, furniture, and even home. They forbid primarily the ownership of the means of production.

Robert Nozick's Libertarian Theory

Nozick offers his reasons for a strong commitment to property rights. Why do we have a strong right to property:

> I conjecture that the answer is connected with the elusive and difficult notion: the meaning of life. A person's shaping his life in accordance with some overall plan is his way of giving meaning to his life; only a being with the capacity to so shape his life can have or strive for a meaningful life (*ASU*, p. 50).

The basis of our right to liberty, including ownership, is this capacity to choose a meaningful life.

Nozick accepts a version of Locke's theory of property and sets forth a rights-based Entitlement Theory of Holdings, involving the principle of justice in acquisition and transfer of holdings. A distribution is just if everyone has that to which he is entitled. To determine what people are entitled to, we must understand what the original position of holdings or possessions was and what constitutes a just transfer of holdings. Borrowing from John Locke's theory of property rights, Nozick argues that we have a right to any possession as long as our ownership does not worsen the position of anyone else. His three principles are:

1. A person who acquires a holding in accordance with the principle of justice in acquisition is entitled to it.

2. A person who acquires a holding in accordance with the principle of justice in transfer, from someone else entitled to the holding, is entitled to the holding.
3. No one is entitled to a holding except by (repeated) application of 1 and 2. (*ASU*, p. 151)

Nozick later adds a principle of rectification of injustice in holdings. If a holding was acquired unjustly, justice requires that it be restored to the original owner. But the basic idea is Lockean. Nozick's Entitlement Theory of Holdings is historical, dependent upon how the acquisition came about. If the original acquisition of property came about by someone appropriating an unowned piece of nature, that person was entitled to it, and could pass it down or transfer it as he so desired, as long as the Lockean proviso was adhered to.

Next Nozick distinguishes between patterned and nonpatterned schemes of distributive justice. "Let us call a principle of distribution patterned if it specifies that a distribution is to vary along with some natural dimension, weighted sum of natural dimensions, or lexicographic ordering of natural dimensions." A patterned principle chooses some trait(s) that indicates how the proper distribution is to be accomplished. It has the form:

To each according to _____.

Different political theories fill in the blank differently. Socialists believe that need is the relevant trait. Meritocrats believe merit is, Desert theorists, desert. Utilitarians, utility. Traditionalists would put class status in the blank. A pluralist might put a combination of traits in the blank, depending on the type of distribution to be made.

Nozick's theory is a nonpatterned scheme. There is no preordained formula to which it must adhere, no pattern it must follow. If it came about justly, the holding is yours, period, and no one has a right to take it away from you.

From each according to what he chooses to do, to each according to what he makes for himself (perhaps with the contracted aid of others) and what others choose to do for him and choose to give him of what they've been given previously (under this maxim) and haven't yet expended or transferred. (*ASU*, p. 160)

Or to state it more succinctly: "From each as they choose, to each as they are chosen."

Nozick's theory maximizes human liberty much in the same way Mill prescribed in his classic treatise, *On Liberty*, advocating laissez-faire capitalism. "The only purpose for which power can be rightfully exercised over any member of a civilized community, against his will, is to prevent harm to others."[3]

Granting people liberty to acquire and transfer property prohibits the government from limiting what they do with their property or from taxing it.

Nozick rejects patterned types of principles, such as those of socialists, meritocrats, and utilitarians, because such attempts to regulate distribution constitute a violation of liberty. Taking liberty seriously would upset patterned distribution schemes. He illustrates this point by considering how a great basketball player, Wilt Chamberlain, could justly upset the patterned balance. Suppose that we have reached a patterned situation of justice based on equality. Imagine that there is a great demand to watch Chamberlain play basketball and that people are willing to pay him an extra 25 cents per ticket in order to see him play. If one million people pay to see him play during the year, the additional gate receipts total $250,000. Chamberlain thus takes home a great deal more than our patterned formula allows, but he seems to have a right to this. Nozick's point is that, in order to maintain a pattern, one must either "continually interfere to stop people from transferring resources as they wish to, or continually interfere to take from some persons resources that others for some reason chose to transfer to them." A socialist or welfarist society would have to "forbid capitalist acts between consenting adults." (*ASU*, pp. 161, 163)

We might well object. "OK, Chamberlain can upset the pattern, but only so far. We, the people, through our elected government, have a right to tax some of that money, so we can use it for the needy." But Nozick has a response: taxation constitutes forced labor, a form of slavery. For consider, suppose I am charged a 25 percent income tax on my earnings. I work a 40-hour week, so I am working 30 hours as a free citizen and 10 hours (25 percent of my time) as a slave to the government. Stephen Kershnar has pointed out that during slavery some owners permitted slaves to work on the shipyards and to keep whatever they made beyond a specific amount, thus providing an incentive to work harder.[4] Taxation is a kind of slavery within an incentive scheme, but it is still slavery, which is exploitation. The free market should be left unregulated and each person be left free to behave as prudently as he or she is able.

A Critical Assessment of Libertarianism

Of course, Nozick and libertarians like F. A. Hayek, Milton Friedman, and John Hospers stress that they are not against private voluntary beneficence to ameliorate the suffering of the poor and needy, who in fact may be victims of an unrestricted free market. But, their opponents point out, there is a problem with private charity, for some beneficent projects may only succeed if they involve large-scale coordinated programs. Consider what is sometimes called the assurance problem. Suppose I am a beneficent individual who wants to support the poor. I see an advertisement for the Voluntary Welfare Fund (VWF), which promises to aid large numbers of the deserving poor. I am inclined to contribute to the VWF, but I reason: *either* a sufficient number of others will contribute to the collective effort to make the project successful, even if I don't contribute to it, *or* not enough others will contribute to it even if I do contribute to it. Since my contribution is small relative to what is needed (though it represents a considerable sacrifice on my part), the probability that my input will make a difference is low. But if it is low, then it is rational for me to withhold my contribution from the VFW. But if others are thinking this way, the worthy project, which we all believe in, will not get the needed support, and the poor will go unaided. So a government enforced program of taxation may be needed to coordinate the goodwill of morally concerned, but rational, individuals. Adam Smith, the father of modern capitalism and a believer in market freedom, put the matter this way, pointing out the Three Duties of Government:

> All systems either of preference or of restraint, therefore, being thus completely taken away, the obvious and simple system of natural liberty establishes itself of its own accord. Every man, as long as he does not violate the laws of justice, is left perfectly free to pursue his own interest his own way, and to bring both his industry and capital into competition with those of any other man, or order of men. . . . According to the system of natural liberty, the sovereign has only three duties to attend to; three duties of great importance, indeed but plain and intelligible to common understandings: first, the duty of protecting the society from the violence and invasion of other independent societies; secondly, the duty of protecting, as far as possible, every member of the society from the injustice or oppression of every other member of it, or the duty of establishing an exact administration of justice; and, thirdly, the duty of erecting and maintaining certain public works and certain public institutions, which it can never be for the interest of any individual, or small number of individuals, to erect and maintain; because the profit could never repay the expense to any individual or small number of individuals, though it may frequently do much more than repay it to a great society.[5]

Libertarians like Nozick agree that government may tax us to carry out its first two duties, provide for an army to defend us from external attack, and provide for a police force and legal system to protect us from internal violence and fraud. But they sometimes neglect or reject the third duty, to which Smith draws our attention. There simply are some vitally beneficial projects too costly for a small number of individuals to carry out successfully, which the government can and should carry out. Examples of these are a national military force, state and local police, mail service, state and federal highways, public education, a sanitation system, and environmental protection, including pollution control. Even libertarians shy away from a policy of private ownership of the roads and highways, whereby drivers would pay tolls to local highway property owners every few miles. These seem reasonable, but why, the critic asks, can't it also carry out a more extensive welfare scheme? Granted, there are many types of welfare schemes, many of which are not justified by good moral reasoning, so these institutions need to be carefully devised, but to preclude them in the way modern libertarians do seems unwarrantedly dogmatic. Smith's broader vision of government's duties within a free-market framework poses a pragmatic challenge to libertarians. Paying one's taxes can be seen as an expression of gratitude for a system that protects us from force, fraud, and pollution, and enhances our lives by providing public sanitation, basic education, and a welfare safety net for those who through no fault of their own end up unemployed or destitute.

Because it assumes a questionably atomistic view of human nature, libertarianism, such as evinced in Nozick's argument comparing taxation with forced labor, seems implausible. The truth is, in the words of the poet John Donne, "No man is an island, entire of itself." Mammals live in groups, and this is especially true of human beings. We are social and political animals. We are nurtured by mothers, reared and socialized in families by parents and siblings and relatives. We are taught a language and a set of customs. We are educated into a culture, internalizing a tradition of myths, symbols, and history. We acquire social and academic skills that enable us to navigate through the labyrinthine maze of a complex, interpersonal world.

Think of all the things we daily use but take for granted that are the result of other people's inventions and contributions to our lives, not to mention the obvious inventions of the wheel, electricity, the incandescent lightbulb, the internal combustion engine, clean running water, indoor plumbing, sanitation systems to filter sewage, and insulated buildings. Then there are the social institutions that help give our lives meaning and protect us from oppression, violence, and disease: the law, a just judicial system, the police, the army, morality itself, codes of etiquette and moral conduct, hospitals and related medical knowledge, agricultural institutions and regulating agencies that enforce safe standards. No one of us is sufficient in him or herself for all the contingencies of life. We are interdependent. We are all in each other's debt.

In a thousand ways each day, the "self-made man" is beholden to the composite and cooperative efforts of a myriad of predecessors who reach back into primitive times and thousands of contemporaries who add support to his life, but whose noncooperation could ruin it. Think of how just nineteen terrorists shook our world and disabused us of our illusions of invulnerability on September 11, 2001. We need each other. We are all part of a social nexus, an intricate, complex web of social and economic ties that bind us together. In such an interconnected web of relations, is it too much to ask each member to contribute a proportionate fraction of his or her income to help maintain the overall social system? The very liberty that enables us to enjoy a large measure of independence and affluence is predicated on social cooperation, and social cooperation in a society like ours, where there are wide gaps in wealth and income, seems to require tax-contributions from its members in order to meet basic needs and provide fair equal opportunity. Those who benefit most from the underlying structures of our society should contribute most. A fair system of taxation is, ideally, both an expression of gratitude for the benefits of community and civilization and an acknowledgment that many people require aid through no fault of their own.

A second problem with the libertarian philosophy is its virtual fetishism over property. They argue from the fact that we own our own bodies to the conclusion that no one should interfere with any of our property, but an absence of argument haunts their theory. It's a far cry from self-ownership to monopoly ownership or ownership of vast tracts of land while others are homeless and landless. The Lockean would argue that, as good stewards, we are not allowed to waste, so that some of our property ought to be used for the welfare of the less fortunate. The utilitarian would argue that property, up to a point, can promote well-being, but that via the principle of diminishing marginal utility, wealth should be redistributed to where it does more good.

There seems to be a disturbing paradox in Nozick's libertarianism. On the one hand, he argues that the right to own property is absolute. The government may not interfere to tax you (except where you have consented to be taxed—for example, for military or police protection). On the other hand, property is necessary for carrying out one's projects toward constructing a meaningful life. But if it is necessary, then, since resources are limited already in the hands of the rich, one would expect some provision to be made for redistributing some wealth so that the propertyless can have a sufficient opportunity to create a meaningful life.

There is a third problem with Nozick's theory. If we were to take the historical acquisition premise seriously, we would probably find it doubtful whether the ownership of most or any of the property owned in the world is justified. A great deal of it was appropriated not through the original mixing of labor, but by military invasion, plunder, violence, and fraud. On Nozick's principles we would have to give much of the land in the United States back to the descendants of the Native Americans who were here first and from whom much of the land was taken. Perhaps most present ownership of land has a sordid history of exploitation or unjust aggression. If this is the case, it may be wiser, let alone more moral, to have a reasonably generous policy toward land use and property, accepting our responsibility to aid those in need.

These, then, are the main problems with libertarianism. It underestimates our interdependence, it overemphasizes property rights, and its logic leads to a quest for an original ownership that may be as elusive or absurd as the quest for the Holy Grail. Many libertarians recognize these problems and try to accommodate them in different ways.

Liberty and the Tragedy of the Commons

In assessing the strengths and weaknesses of libertarianism, let us look further into the value and abuses of liberty. Liberty can be abused, so that what may seem to be an exercise of freedom may turn out to be a massive catastrophe, diminishing each of our liberties. This process, developed in recent years by the ecologist Garrett Hardin, is called the *Tragedy of the Commons*. Imagine a public field (a "commons") where farmers have been grazing their cows for centuries. Because of the richness of the field and the poverty of the farmers, the field is never overgrazed. Now there comes a time when the carrying capacity of the field is reaching its limit. At this point, it is in the short-term rational self-interest of each farmer to add one more cow to the commons in spite of its limitations. The farmer reasons that by grazing yet one more cow, he will be gaining a positive factor of 1 (the value of the extra cow) and losing only a fraction of the negative unit 1, the loss of the field's resources, since all of the farmers share that equally whether or not they participate in overgrazing. So it is in each farmer's interest to overgraze, but if too many farmers act in this way it soon will be against their interest, for the pasture will be ruined. Hence the tragedy of the commons! Complete liberty, complete disaster! A comparable tragedy is occurring in our use of natural resources. We are in danger of depleting the world's resources through wanton overuse. Similarly, freely engaging in activities that cause greenhouse gases to be released into the atmosphere, has a deleterious effect on the climate patterns. To prevent such a tragedy, we must have mutually agreed upon, mutually coercive laws that govern matters such as population increase, overgrazing, overfishing, deforestation, pollution, and the like. Each nation must limit its liberty and manage its own commons, and if one fails to do so, the logic continues, it must be left to its own misery. Benevolent intervention on the part of misguided do-gooders is only likely to increase the overall misery, as such intervention encourages continued waste and neglect, discourages needed reform measures, and only delays the massive starvation that will eventually catch up with the nation. This is known as the Ratchet effect.

Russell Roberts has pointed out that a similar process goes on in government spending.[6] Take the members of Congress. They typically get elected on the basis of promising to obtain federal funds for their districts. District A is made up of farmers, so Representative A gets legislation passed to subsidize the farmers in A. Federal taxes are raised to cover the subsidy. Everyone in A is pleased. But District B needs a new fine arts theater, so Representative B introduces a bill giving B funds or a new theater. It passes, the theater is built, and everyone in District B is happy. District C, because of increasing traffic congestion, could use a four-lane highway bypass, so Representative C introduces legislation to send millions of dollars to his district and the bill passes. Everyone in C is happy. And so representatives of all the hundreds of other congressional districts play the same game, many for very good causes, some for not-so-good causes, but the system encourages waste. Each district and its representative reasons: because we're only paying a fraction of the cost for project P, we should ask for the maximum amount of money to carry out this project. "The government is paying, not us." But who is the government? Because every district is thinking the same way, the result is extravagant costs and much waste. This is not an argument against helping the needy or funding worthy projects or giving emergency aid to districts that have experienced a natural disaster. But it illustrates a problem in representative democracy, where politicians are rewarded for bringing tax dollars to their districts. Note, for example, a partial list of government subsidies: sugar, tobacco, corn, peanut, cotton, and mohair. Although these subsidies have all been enacted by Congress, it's doubtful whether any of these programs are generally beneficial to the American people. Instead, they benefit small special interest groups, but they are powerful enough to gain the support of individual congressmen. Some defenders argue that the system is justified because it evens things out. We each give something and get something equivalent. But even if we all did benefit, this logic overlooks the vast expenditures needed to support the middlemen, the bureaucrats who collect the taxes, and allocate it to the projects. Wouldn't it make more sense for the district that wanted the theater or bypass to raise the funds themselves and not burden others with its wants? That way there would be an incentive to keep costs down, for the people who benefit are paying for the project. When we all exercise our liberty in demanding more resources, the tragedy of the commons occurs, eventually bringing ruination, the total loss of liberty, to all. By siphoning off tax dollars to everyone's benefit, we end up harming everyone. Individual liberty turns out to be collective irrationality.

Conclusion

The strength of libertarianism is its emphasis on personal liberty. Libertarians have a point in emphasizing the value of liberty and warning of the dangers of governmental intervention in our lives. Governments can become oppressive by imposing heavy taxes on people. Elected representatives often remain in power by directing government revenues to local constituencies. But when every representative begins to think this way, the cumulative effect is a tragedy of the commons, where the system is endangered.

The libertarian also cautions us about compromising our capitalist, free-enterprise system, a system that is predicated on allowing free-market exchanges. Such a system has proved to be the best means for lifting societies out of poverty into abundance. Other systems, such as socialism or welfare liberalism, may look attractive, but they are fraught with great risk, if not our economic doom.

There is an ancient tale of a dog with a bone in his mouth who looked down into a pool of water. There he saw a reflection of a dog with a large bone in his mouth—a bone that looked larger than the one he had. Eager to have the better bone, he opened his mouth and started after the better bone. The bone he had fell out of his mouth and was lost forever. The libertarian conservatively warns: before you go after a "better" political ideology, make sure it's worth risking the bone you already have. It may turn out to be an illusion, an exaggerated reflection of what you already have.

Notes

1. Robert Nozick, *Anarchy, State and Utopia* (New York: Basic Books, 1974), p. 174.

2. J. Rousseau, *Discourse on the Origins of Inequality* (Reprinted in Pojman, *Political Philosophy* (New York: McGraw-Hill, 2002).

3. John Stuart Mill, *On Liberty*, 1859.

4. Stephen Keshnar pointed this out in correspondence in October 2003.

5. Adam Smith, *The Wealth of Nations* (New York: Random House, 1937), p. 651.

6. Russell Roberts, "If You're Paying, I'll Have Sirloin," *Wall Street Journal*, April 1998.

CHAPTER 4

The Liberal Theory of Justice: John Rawls

> All social primary goods—liberty and opportunity, income and wealth, and the bases of self-respect—are to be distributed equally unless an unequal distribution of any or all of these goods is to the advantage of the least favored.
>
> (*A Theory of Justice*, 1971 [henceforth *TJ*], p. 303)

John Rawls's Theory of Justice as Fairness

In John Rawls's theory of Justice as Fairness, we have what is probably the most important contribution to political philosophy in the twentieth century, one with which both friends and foes must come to terms. Stuart Hampshire called it "the most substantial and interesting contribution to moral philosophy since the [Second World] War [wherein] the substance of a critical and liberal political philosophy is argued with an assurance and breadth of mind that puts the book in the tradition of Adam Smith and Mill and Sidgwick."[1] Robert Nisbett calls it the "long awaited successor to Rousseau's Social Contract, the Rock on which the Church of Equality can properly be founded in our time." In scope and power, it rivals the classics of Hobbes, Locke, and Rousseau. Deservedly, no philosophical work in the last quarter of a century has been quoted or debated more than this one. Fundamentally egalitarian (see quotation above), it seeks to justify the welfare state. Rawls accepts that liberal ideas of justice can only be justified where the "circumstances of justice" obtain, that is, in a situation of relative affluence like those in Western nations. In his second book, *Political Liberalism* (Harvard, 1994), he clarifies his position as attempting to provide political stability. He recognizes our society as "a cooperative venture for mutual advantage" (*TJ*, 4). A modern society is pluralistic, made up of vastly different worldviews with competing conceptions of the good. What Justice as Fairness aims to do is provide the ground rules for an overlapping consensus, the set of minimal, noncontroversial principles on which we can all agree and which ensure political stability (sufficient motivation to comply with and support the basic institutions of a society over time).

Rawls's theory is deontological, distinguishing itself from utilitarian rivals by its focus on meeting individual needs rather than on aggregate or average welfare.

Each person possesses an inviolability founded on justice that even the welfare of society as a whole cannot override. For this reason justice denies that the loss of freedom for some is made right by a greater good shared by others. It does not allow that the sacrifices imposed on a few are outweighed by the larger sum of advantages enjoyed by the many. Therefore, in a just society the liberties of equal citizenship are taken as settled; the rights secured by justice are not subject to political bargaining or the calculus of social interests. (*TJ*, p. 3)

Rawls is an egalitarian, one who believes that each minimally rational human being (sometimes called a "person"), who has a conception of the good and is able to act justly is valuable, and equally so.

It seems reasonable to suppose that the parties in the original position are equal. That is, all have the same rights in the procedure for choosing principles; each can make proposals, submit reasons for their acceptance, and so on. Obviously the purpose of these conditions is to represent equality between human beings as moral persons, as creatures having a conception of their good and capable of a sense of justice. The basis of equality is taken to be similarity in these two respects. Systems of ends are not ranked in value; and each man is presumed to have the requisite ability to understand and act upon whatever principles are adopted. Together with the veil of ignorance, these conditions define the principles of justice as those which rational persons concerned to advance their interests would consent to as equals when none are known to be advantaged or disadvantaged by social and natural contingencies (*TJ*, p. 19).

Rawls employs what he calls wide Reflective Equilibrium in order to arrive at the correct comprehensive moral and political theory. That is, we begin by proposing hypothetical theories and then testing them against our most fixed and definite intuitions about moral particulars. If a theory does not accommodate our fixed intuitions, we modify or even reject (or revise) it in favor of a theory that does. For example, suppose we begin with a form of classical utilitarianism and test it against the fixed intuition that slavery is wrong or that it is wrong to convict an innocent person for a crime even if it will minimize suffering (say, by staving off a race riot). We see that instituting slavery might maximize utility and, likewise, framing, convicting, and punishing an innocent man for a crime might also do that by staving off a riot. Since utilitarianism fails to accommodate our deep intuitions, we reject utilitarianism and try another theory until we find one where our intuitions and theory accommodate each other. In rare cases we might modify our intuitions if we think that the theory is worth saving. Rawls uses Reflective Equilibrium to reject theories like utilitarianism and perfectionism (i.e., the theory that the state should promote a definite thick theory of the Good), but it may be instructive to apply it to his own theory as well.

Justice as Fairness is in its formative stage, in Nozick's term, nonpatterned, in that it doesn't reward according to any specific criterion, such as desert, contribution, or need, though need plays an important role in the system. Rawls agrees with Nozick that patterned versions of justice are faulty, and agrees that maximal liberty is a social requirement, but he disagrees with libertarian views like Nozick's, which make negative liberty into an absolute value. Instead, Rawls presents a version of the social contract that is broadly Kantian, in which a theory of just procedures takes the place of substantive principles. Rawls holds that if fair procedures govern the conditions of choice, whatever principles are chosen will be fair ones, since in the contract tradition, justice simply is whatever rational choosers decide on in fair conditions. But while the initial stage of the choosers is nonpatterned, the second stage, consisting in the policy chosen, is patterned.

In *A Theory of Justice*, Rawls sets forth a hypothetical contract theory in which the bargainers in the original position go behind a veil of ignorance in order to devise a set of fundamental agreements that will govern society. "Certain principles of justice are justified because they would be agreed upon in a situation of equality" (*TJ*, p. 21). Behind the metaphorical veil no one knows his or her place in society, class, gender, race, religion, generation, social status, fortune in the distribution of natural assets and abilities, or even intelligence. They do not know their conception of the good. That is, each of us has a different idea of what makes life worth living, based on our moral or religious or aesthetic theories. The millionaire business executive has a different conception of the good from the school teacher, the farmer, or the Trappist monk. This information, making up the thick theory of the good, could influence the contractor's deliberation, so it must be withheld. Those in the original position do have basic psychological knowledge about human nature, and have a common "thin theory" of the good. That is, they know the "primary goods," the liberties, opportunities, wealth, income, and social bases of self-respect. These are fundamental values, for whatever else people want, they will rationally want these basic goods. The capitalist, the monk, the dancer, the garbage collector, and the philosopher will all value liberty and self-respect and adequate wealth. Parties to the contract are to act as mutually disinterested (i.e., they don't envy others their good fortune), rationally self-interested agents, and choose the basic principles that will govern their society. By denying individuals knowledge of their natural assets and social position, Rawls prevents them from exploiting their advantages, thus transforming a decision under risk (where probabilities of outcomes are known) to a decision under uncertainty (where probabilities are not known). To the question, Why should the individual acknowledge the principles chosen in the original position as morally binding? Rawls would answer, We should abide by these principles because we all would choose them under fair conditions. That is, as long as the procedure is fair, we must accept the results as fair.

Rawls thinks that these conditions in the original position ensure objectivity and impartiality of judgment. If you don't know any significant facts about your particular identity, you will be less likely to be biased in your favor. You will resemble the ideal of the blindfolded Justice who is committed to balancing the scales, only you are to do so from a self-interested point of view. Think of the U.S. Supreme Court justices who had to decide whether the Florida electoral vote in the 2000 presidential election—which was challenged by the Democratic constituencies—was fair. Many people believed the justices were biased in making their controversial 5 to 4 decision according to ideological lines. Suppose we had a drug that would cause people to forget their party loyalties and particular interests, but remain rational agents. We could have given it to the justices and have expected a different voting pattern. Perhaps there would have been near unanimity one way or the other rather than a narrow decision.

One further requirement of this hypothetical contract is that the contractors, as rational choosers, are to maximize the minimal position one could fall into, choosing the arrangements "as though your enemy were to assign you a place in society." Rawls calls this the maximin principle. He argues that the rational chooser will pick a system where, in a reasonably affluent society, you will do relatively well even on the bottom of the social-economic ladder. Putting this in monetary terms (to simplify), we can imagine three types of societies each with three economic classes (Table 4.1).

Which society would it be rational to choose? Classical Utilitarians would choose Society 1, for it maximizes utility, giving the highest aggregate. However, Rawls thinks we will reject this alternative, since we are concerned to maximize not aggregate utility, but the worst off position, and since we are choosing under uncertainty and have no way of ensuring that we won't end up at the bottom. So applying the *maximin* strategy, the rational person would choose Society 3, though it has the lowest aggregate and the lowest average utility. But if you're the worst off in society, you will be better off than if you were in Society 1 or 2. Rawls has been criticized for being too conservative here. Rational choosers might gamble and choose a society with a higher chance of doing better. One could also opt for an average utilitarian position, by calculating expected utility to be had in each society by summing up the amounts of welfare of all the people and dividing by the number. The society that offered the highest expected utility would be the one with the highest expected average utility, and would thus be chosen. One could also follow R. M. Hare's modified utilitarian suggestion and provide a welfare safety net, ensuring that everyone's basic needs are met, but then allowing individuals to advance their economic and social positions as far beyond the mean as was possible. This is the rationale of most social systems in Western Europe. There is no ceiling on income, but the poor are assured of a minimum below which they will not be allowed to fall. The principle of economic efficiency, Pareto Optimality,[2] which holds that an advancement in economic gain is optimal if no one is made worse off by it, would favor Hare's approach. It would seem to favor

TABLE 4.1

Society 1	Society 2	Society 3
$70,000	$50,000	$40,000
$50,000	$5,000	$20,000
$4,000	$35,000	$10,000

TABLE 4.2

		Citizen A	Citizen B
Units of Primary Goods	I	10 units	10 units
	II	15 units	50 units
	III	10 units	100 units

the notion of giving people incentives to work hard. Consider the following scheme (Table 4.2) of distributing primary goods. If citizen B, by gaining 40 more units (situation II), will raise the worse off citizen A's allotment by 5 points, Rawls's maximin principle would allow B's advancement, but it would not allow situation III in which B's advancement was to 100 units, since this doesn't raise A's allotment. The Pareto Principle would permit B's advancement, since no one is worse off and one person is better off.

It seems rational to choose a society that permits the third row of distributions to occur. Or consider a counterexample given by Russell Keat and David Miller. Suppose "a starving man has to choose which of two boxes to open, on the basis of the following information: the first contains two loaves of bread; the second may contain a single loaf, or it may be packed with food—he is told nothing about the relative likelihood of each of these outcomes."[3] Would it not seem rational to choose the second box, since it does contain at least the minimum amount to stave off starvation and may contain a great bonus? Rawls seems committed to choosing the first box. We will discuss this problem further below, but the motivation for Rawls's conservatism here is his concern for political stability. That is, he seeks to provide a motivation for adherence to the rules that govern society. I know that no matter how bleak my life chances become, society's institutions, representatives, and rules are working together to enhance my well-being. Thus, I will have a sufficient reason for supporting the society.

The Principles

Rawls calls his system "Justice As Fairness" because he seeks a contract on whose fairness all parties will agree. In effect, the parties to the contract should choose the kind of principles they could live with if their enemies were assigning them positions in society. Rawls argues that they would choose the following two principles:

1. Everyone will have an equal right to the most extensive basic liberties compatible with similar liberty for others.
2. Social and economic inequalities must satisfy two conditions:

   (a) They are to the greatest benefit of the least advantaged ("the difference principle").

(b) They are attached to positions open to all under conditions of fair equality of opportunity. (*TJ*, pp. 302–3)

These principles are to be arranged in lexical order: First, 1: Equal extensive liberty for all. Second, 2(b): Equal Opportunity to all positions in the society. In order to achieve this, income and resources would need to be redistributed from those who have abundance to those who have inadequate resources. Finally, 2(a): Arrangements that apply the Difference Principle, permitting inequalities if and only if they redound to the benefit of the worst-off.

The controversial principle is 2(a), the Difference Principle. Rawls subsumes it under the ideal of fraternity, of "not wanting to have greater advantages unless this is to the benefit of others who are less well off" (*TJ*, p. 105). He likens it to the relationship in a family where members do not wish to gain unless they do so in ways that advance the interests of the other members. You would be assured that if you ended up on the social bottom, everything was being done to raise your prospects, that your condition was a priority.

Rawls would like to distribute resources equally, but he sees two problems. First, unless a high level of goods is available in society, equality at a subsistence or mediocre level of affluence is not desirable, so we should encourage economic disparities if that will enable the bottom to rise. "A rising tide raises all ships." The second problem is related to this. Socialist programs enforcing equal distributions undermine incentive. Most people will work harder if they believe they will have a more affluent life as a result. Rawls seeks to capitalize on this truth by tying economic advancement to raising the position of the worst off members of the society. Finally, as we noted earlier in this chapter, Rawls rejects the notion of desert as applicable to social justice. No one deserves his greater natural capacity nor merits a more favorable starting place in society. "The notion of desert seems not to apply" to cases where one person achieves greater ability or status in society. Natural talents, in a sense, are a common asset, collectively owned.[4] Justice, according to Rawls, rejects the notion of preinstitutional desert—rewards or status that is due to us by virtue of our abilities, achievements, merit, or effort.

An Assessment of Rawls's Theory of Justice as Fairness

Because of its prominence, Rawls's theory has been subject to countless scrutiny from all sides of the political spectrum. We shall briefly discuss three of the more prominent criticisms, including some further problems with the difference principle.

1. Rawls has been criticized by communitarians like Michael Sandel for leaving his contractors behind the veil of ignorance without personal identity, as mere abstract, thin men.

   Rawls' principles do not mention moral desert because, strictly speaking, no one can be said to deserve anything . . . On Rawls' view people have no intrinsic worth, no worth that is intrinsic in the sense that it is theirs prior to or independent of . . . what just institutions attribute to them.[5]

By subtracting all their contingent traits, he's left only the shell of a person. This criticism seems unfair. What Rawls is doing is setting forth an ideal condition of impartial judgment, as we expect in umpires in baseball games and referees in basketball games. This idea of impartiality, set forth in our opening quotation of Chapter 1 by Stanley Benn, seems necessary for all rational thinking. We want to ensure fairness as well as justice, so I think Rawls can meet this criticism.

2. A second criticism, set forth by Wallace Matson, is that Rawls confuses fairness with justice. Rawls seems misleading in characterizing justice as a kind of fairness, for these two concepts are distinct. Fairness is comparative, whereas justice is noncomparative. A law may be unjust but fair in that it is applied consistently. I may give you a grade lower than what you deserve, say a C instead of a B, but since I similarly downgrade all my students, I am still treating you fairly, though unjustly. It was said of the great Green Bay Packers football coach, Vince Lombardi, that he treated his players equally, treating them all like dogs. Since they were human beings, not dogs, Lombardi treated them unjustly but fairly. Similarly, the notion of a fair wage is not the same thing as a just wage. If I pay men $15 per hour for a job that I pay women only $10 per hour, I am unfair, but if I pay them both only $10 per hour when they deserve more, I am unjust, but not unfair.[6]

3. A Critique of the Difference Principle. As we have already noted, Rawls's difference principle and its associate, the maximin principle, can be challenged. Rawls may well be correct in elevating need to a canon of justice and recognizing that in an affluent society like ours, the government should do more than simply promote negative liberty. It should also redistribute some wealth to the worst off, ensuring that their basic needs are met. Meeting needs is a controversial subject, for it's not always clear what a basic need is. Surely, having sufficient nourishment, shelter, and clothing are basic needs. In our society, having a basic education is also a basic need. In many communities, having an automobile or a radio may be a basic need, so what counts as a basic need in many cases seems to be relative to the social context. But, as we noted earlier, a threshold welfare principle, providing a safety net for those with unmet basic needs may produce more social stability and utility than the deliverances of the difference principle.

Rawls seems correct over against Nozick and libertarians in recognizing that justice includes meeting basic needs. Rawls may, however, go too far in correcting for that neglect, underappreciating the need for personal responsibility and desert. Citizens must be held accountable for their actions and should be rewarded and punished accordingly. Why should the freeloader get any welfare if he doesn't contribute to the common good, let alone pull his own weight? But this leads to the most significant problem in Rawls's theory: the downplaying of the role of desert in a theory of justice, to which we now turn.

On Rawls's Rejection of Preinstitutional Desert

For Rawls justice precedes desert and not the other way around. There is no *prejusticial* desert. As we noted in Chapter 2, Joel Feinberg makes a distinction between preinstitutional or *natural* desert and *institutional* desert.[7] Natural desert entails giving people what they ought to receive even if no institutions exist to give them what they ought to receive. Institutional desert, on the other hand, entails giving people what they deserve based on an institutional framework with rules defining what people should receive. An example of institutional desert is a contractual relationship in which an employer promises you so much money for so much work. The rules give you a *right* or *entitlement* to that money, if you have done the work. Prizes, rewards, and grades are all examples of institutional desert. As we saw in Chapter 2, the classical conception of desert holds that one ought to receive benefits or burdens according to one's effort, contribution, or meritorious performance. A strong institutional conception of desert reduces desert to entitlements and holds that where there is no set of rules, there is no basis for distribution of benefits and burdens. Effort and merit are legitimate criteria for distribution only if there is an institutional structure determining that they are the relevant criteria for distribution. The institutional arrangement could make need or interest or utility or some other quality the relevant criterion.

John Rawls supports the idea of institutional desert and rejects the idea of natural desert.

> It seems to be one of the fixed points of our considered judgments that no one deserves his place in the distribution of native endowments, any more than one deserves one's initial starting place in society. (*TJ*, 104)

Since no one deserves his natural endowments, Rawls argues, no one deserves the benefits that his abilities enable him to acquire. Just because you're smarter and more talented than I am and hence can produce more goods, you have no basis for claiming a right to superior wealth or benefits. Furthermore, even if it is not your talents but your superior work habits, your work ethic, that enables you to outperform me, that cannot be the basis for distribution.

> The assertion that a man deserves the superior character that enables him to make the effort to cultivate his abilities is equally problematic; for his character depends in large part upon fortunate family and social circumstances for which he can claim no credit. The notion of desert seems not to apply to these cases.

From this Rawls concludes that "the more advantaged representative man cannot say that he deserves and therefore has a right to a scheme of cooperation in which he is permitted to acquire benefits in ways that do not contribute to the welfare of others." The implication is that unless rewarding you for your hard, successful work is a result of social rules based on social utility, you have no claim on rewards for your work.

It seems that Rawls is appealing to a deterministic interpretation of human nature. We, with our native abilities, are the products of our heredity and environment. Genetic endowment and family upbringing made us what we are "for which [we] can claim no credit." The argument seems to be that since we don't deserve our natural abilities, including our work ethic, we don't deserve what we produce through our abilities and work ethic. But this seems a *non sequitur*. Just because I don't deserve my talents doesn't entail that I don't deserve the benefits that I obtain through using my talents.[8]

Only when an institutional system is set up can we have a distributional scheme.

> It is perfectly true that given a just system of cooperation as a scheme of public rules and expectations set up by it, those who, with the respect of improving their condition, have done what the system announces that it will reward are entitled to their advantages. In this sense the more fortunate have a claim to their better situation; their claims are legitimate expectations established by social institutions, and the community is obliged to meet them (*TJ*, 103).

Rawls reduces all talk of desert to that of *entitlements* and *legitimate expectations*. It is the language of rights. If the state permits you to have a tax write-off for an additional child, you are entitled to that write-off. If society has a social welfare system for the poor and you are poor, you have a right to that welfare. Rawls mainly confines his discussion to distribution of goods, but he seems to accept a notion of natural desert when it comes to punishment for crimes. He acknowledges that we have natural duties that, if violated, require fitting punishment. If we applied his doctrine of institutional desert to crime and punishment, we would have to say that we have a right to punish a murderer only if there is a law against murder. By this logic, if there is no law against murder or lying or cheating, then one is entitled to murder or lie or cheat.

We would say in the case of punishment that Rawls has things backwards. It is not because murder, lying, and cheating are institutionally prohibited that they are wrong; but because they are morally wrong that they should be institutionally prohibited (made illegal) and should be punished. There seems to be a sense of natural justice that operates in cases of crime and punishment so that the punishment ought to fit the crime, the worse the crime, the worse the punishment. I think Rawls agrees with this rationale.

It would seem that Rawls needs a broader sense of desert for his own theory. He wants to hold people, as autonomous agents, responsible for their actions. But if I am responsible for my actions, then I must be said to deserve praise or blame, depending on the moral nature of those actions. But this seems to presuppose a conception of natural desert. It may be that until society recognizes certain moral norms, morality is simply an idea, but even in this presocial state, morality has validity as the ideal set of rules that rational people would choose to govern their social conduct. Rawls wants to preserve the dignity of humanity, but for that he needs a robust sense of responsibility, not simply rights. But to have a robust sense of responsibility entails a notion of desert.

The classic notion that justice is giving people what they independently deserve is replaced by the notion that people deserve what justice (institutionally) dictates. Rawls should say more about his rejection of desert. As I argued in the first section of this chapter, he seems to hold that since we are all determined by heredity and environmental conditions, especially our family upbringing, we don't deserve the results of our endeavors. Our talents are the result of a natural and social lottery. Since we can't take credit for any of our talents, virtues, or vices, we can't take credit for what we do with our talents or virtues. At other times, Rawls seems to say that it's just impracticable to take desert into account. Now that we are coming to the close of our discussion of Rawls's notion of justice, we can ask the question raised in the first section: Is it true that desert cannot function as a principle of justice? Giving up desert isn't without serious consequences for morality and autonomy, concepts Rawls surely wants to keep. But if we're autonomous agents, then don't we deserve the consequences of our actions? Rawls seems to agree that if I intentionally injure someone without justification or murder someone, I should be punished for it—because I deserve to be punished—not simply because it may deter crime? Note, doesn't Rawls' own system that those who benefit the worst off be allowed to keep their advantage of goods depend on a notion of desert? Don't they deserve to keep their extra resources because they have benefited the worst off, fulfilling the condition of the Difference Principle?

Furthermore, Rawls wants us to respect ourselves and others, but respect can't be given by fiat—it must be earned. We must believe we are worthy of respect, that we deserve it. We may disagree as to the exact place of desert in the constitution of justice, whether it can exist alone or must be balanced by the concept of need or even rights, but it is an ineliminable feature of any plausible conception of justice. That Rawls fails to appreciate these points certainly undermines his project. But his theory may be revised to incorporate a desert provision and thus survive. He makes the point that it is often impracticable to reward on the basis of desert. But even this may be an exaggeration. Don't we take desert into consideration in deciding whether the accused is guilty of the crime? We may not be able to do this with the exactness we would like, but the concept of *mens rea* is a well-established quality in determining guilt or innocence in criminal trials. We can often base our rewards or praise on this feature too. If a person makes every effort to obtain skills in order to get a job, we deem him more worthy of our help than someone who doesn't. Certainly, in close communities, we make these judgments all the time, holding people accountable for their actions. If we apply this notion of desert to the difference principle, it has the effect of modifying its application. Some of the worst off may not deserve to be given more primary goods, so we have no obligation to them beyond minimal maintenance. As already noted, Rawls omits a sustained discussion of punishment. But, we may ask, aren't criminals deserving of their "worst off" status in prison? Similarly, some of the needy may not deserve to be helped. We may help them out of mercy and kindness, but that is not justice, but benevolence.

What may be true is that justice doesn't consist merely in requiting desert. Need may also be a relevant canon of distribution of resources. Perhaps in a generally affluent society like ours, distributive justice consists of a combination of meeting needs and requiting desert.

If we apply Rawls's own Principle of Reflective Equilibrium to his theory of Justice as Fairness, we might well decide that it needs to be revised, if not altogether rejected. For desert and merit seem to be fixed points in our common consciousness, without which it is hard to make sense of responsibility, and these principles have little or no place in Rawls's theory. Perhaps merit has a minor place in that one could argue that, according to Rawls's formulation of the difference principle, those who, in the process of attaining high social positions or wealth, bring up the worst off, merit their superior status. However, this seems a rather tepid and inadequate concession to merit, for we normally think that merit is more worthy than this, reaching into almost every aspect of social life where appraisal is important, from assigning grades in class to hiring airplane pilots and promoting professors and generals. At least as basic an intuition is our sense that desert should enter into our scheme of justice, so that only the guilty should be punished, and sometimes the worst off are where they are due to their own fault, and so may deserve to be poorly off. We may still have obligations to the undeserving, to rehabilitate them, but they are a different sort of obligation than we have to the deserving poor.

Samuel Scheffler has set forth a defense of Rawls's position.[9] He argues that Rawls accepts a place for natural desert with regard to retributive justice, but not distributive justice. This is because retributive justice is individualistic, whereas distributive justice is holistic.

> With Desert an application may apply to the individual act apart from the whole, but the principles of distributive Justice do not apply to a single transaction in isolation or apart from the whole. This holism derives in part from "a strong sense of the equal worth of persons and from a firm conviction that in a just society all citizens must enjoy equal standing. It also derives from a conviction that, in the circumstances of moderate scarcity of resources that are typical of human societies, citizens' material prospects are profoundly interconnected through their shared and effectively unavoidable participation in a set of fundamental practices and institutions—the economy, legal system, the political framework—that establish and enforce the ground rules of social cooperation. People's prospects are seen as connected in at least three ways. First, people's productive contributions are mutually dependent on the contributions of others. Second, the economic value of people's talents is socially determined in the sense that it depends both on the number of people with similar talents and on the needs, preferences, and the choices of others. Third, people's expectations of material gain are linked in the sense that virtually any decision to assign economic benefits to one person or class has economic implications for the other persons and classes. The holist concludes that, in

light of these moral and empirical considerations, it makes no normative sense to suppose that there could be, at the level of fundamental principle, a standard for assigning such benefits that appealed solely to characteristics of or facts about the proposed beneficiaries. . . . Accordingly, the holist denies that there is any legitimate conception of this kind that is pertinent to questions of economic benefit. Instead, the norms of distributive justice must be thought of as specifying the contours of a fair social framework for the allocation of scarce material resources among citizens of equal worth and standing.[10]

This argument has merit. It is a similar holistic argument to the one we used against Nozick's libertarianism in the last chapter, but it goes too far. First, many distributions, such as jobs and offices, are not strictly economic (such as university professorships, military officers, and leaders of charity organizations), although they may carry economic benefits. Here merit and desert count, not need or equal outcomes. Second, although economics is partly a product of luck, skill (merit) and effort do play a role. The hard-working entrepreneur is more likely to succeed in business than the slothful one. Economic success seems to be a function of luck, effort, skill, and useful contribution. Perhaps a capitalist system honors luck and skill more than effort, whereas, as we said in Chapter 2 while discussing Marx's labor theory of value, a socialist system would tend to place objective worth on the work itself, holding that the carpenter who does a certain amount of work deserves a wage commensurate with the labor value. There are problems with the notion of objective labor value, but it does illustrate that the concept of desert can be applied to economics.

A Reconciling Egalitarianism

Ronald Dworkin has attempted to develop an egalitarianism, which follows Rawls in being egalitarian, but also recognizes the role of responsibility in a more explicit manner. Dworkin holds that each citizen has a right to be treated with equal concern and respect.[11] Dworkin seems to take egalitarianism for granted as a self-evident foundational principle, which doesn't need defense. He images an ideal situation where everyone has the same starting point in life, where the less talented (handicapped) are subsidized by an insurance scheme funded by taxation. In this ideal situation, each person has an equal opportunity to use his or her resources to improve his life. Since natural abilities are a product of the natural lottery, these differences should be equalized by giving special resources to the less talented. But then personal responsibility enters the picture. An egalitarian distribution of goods should offset differences in talent at the starting gate, but it should not offset the differences that result from our effort and free choices. That is, each person should have an equal opportunity to develop his life as he or she sees fit, but no attempt should be made to equalize people once they have freely chosen. In the everyday life of individuals, the free market should be allowed free reign. A natural objection to Dworkin's distinction is that people have differing values and preferences that they have not chosen and so are not responsible for. Jack may simply crave caviar and expensive sports cars, while Jill is content with vegetables and a bicycle.

The economist, Amartya Sen, has attempted to correct this discrepancy by supplementing Dworkin's proposal with a supplementary input of resources to make up for the deficiency of ability in the less talented.[12] Basic nourishment, mobility, education, and the like are so vital to living a fulfilled life that society should redistribute wealth in order to compensate the less able in these respects, so that they are equally able to live a worthwhile life. But both Dworkin and Sen agree that at some point a person must be held responsible for his or her state. Some people, because of superior commitment to their goals and hard work, will succeed in life better than the less committed, and the state should not intervene to correct for these differences in outcomes. Equality of opportunity does not guarantee equality of outcomes. Individuals deserve different amounts of success depending on their choices. Of course, questions remain about exactly how equal opportunity can be instituted in society, for social factors, such as family background and racial discrimination, may create enormous differences in people that are apparently insurmountable in the quest for genuine equal starting points. Genetic factors, determining basic personality type and intelligence, also militate against deep equality of opportunity. But even if we cannot completely overcome natural and acquired differences in life-chances, we may still have an obligation to reduce the differences to a greater degree than we have. However, these post-Rawlsian egalitarians recognize the importance of personal responsibility and its concomitant concept, desert. In this way, they combine a commitment to equality with a commitment to desert. Justice requires that to some significant degree we are accountable for our actions and for how we end up in life.

Conclusion

We have noted Hume's "circumstances of justice," that justice becomes salient in a situation of moderate scarcity where people have limited sympathies. In the last three chapters we have examined three contemporary theories of justice, beginning with the classical notion that justice involves giving people what they deserve, going on to Locke and Nozick's libertarian notion of property rights, and, finally, ending with Rawls's contractarian welfare egalitarianism. We argued that the classic notion of desert, giving people what is their due, while needing qualification, must play some role in both distributive and retributive justice. Each of the theories we have examined has merit, so that it is reasonable to conclude that justice has something to do (1) with allowing people to live their own lives in their own way (libertarianism), (2) with aiding the worst off members of society, meeting their basic needs (assuming they are not undeserving), and (3) with rewarding people according to their desert and merit. We ended this discussion with a brief analysis of the reconciling egalitarians who seek to combine equal opportunity with personal responsibility and desert. This pluralist conception of justice will be further expanded and developed in the next chapter.

Notes

1. Stuart Hampshire, "A New Philosophy of the Just Society," *New York Review of Books* 18:3 (February 24, 1972).

2. A state S1 of a system is *Pareto Optimal* if and only if there is no feasible alternative state System S2, such that at least one individual is better off in S2 than in S1 and no one is worse off in S2 than in S1. Hare's suggestion is in "Rawls' Theory of Justice" in Norman Daniels, ed., *Reading Rawls* (London: Basil Blackwell, 1975). For similar points, see John Harsanyi, *Essays in Ethics, Social Behavior and Scientific Explanation* (Dordrecht: Reidel, 1976); Harry Frankfurt, "Equality as a Moral Ideal," *Ethics*, vol. 98.1 (October 1987).

3. Russell Keat and David Miller, "Understanding Justice," *Political Theory*, 2:1 (February 1974).

4. "The two principles are equivalent, as I have remarked, to an undertaking to regard the distribution of natural abilities as collective assets so that the more fortunate are to benefit only in ways that help those who have lost out." (*TJ*, p. 179. See also p. 101.)

5. Michael Sandel, *Liberalism and the Limits of Justice* (Cambridge University Press, 1982), p. 88.

6. Wallace Matson makes this criticism in several places, including in his "Justice: A Funeral Oration" (in Pojman, *Political Philosophy: Modern and Contemporary Readings* [New York: McGraw-Hill, 2002]). In that article, by a series of imaginative tales Matson contrasts natural justice (the authentic type) over against Rawls's paternalistic justice. The former is "bottom-up" and is based on voluntary agreements, while the latter is "top-down," based on the will of government. In the former, freedom is the starting point and property the necessary good; while in the latter equality is the goal and the government effectively owns all property. The mistake of paternalistic or top-down justice is to suppose that the love and egalitarianism of the family can be extended to society at large. Matson illustrates the tension between these two motifs that exists in the philosophy of John Rawls, who with his first principle of liberty expresses bottom-up justice, but with his second "difference" principle—which distributes all inequalities in favor of the parties that are worst off—expresses top-down, paternalistic justice.

7. Joel Feinberg, "Justice and Personal Desert," *Nomos VI Justice*, eds. C. J. Friedich and John W. Chapman (New York: Atherton, 1963), pp. 63–97.

8. In another place (*TJ*, 312), Rawls says that rewarding moral worth is simply impractical. That is, there are enormous epistemic problems in determining just what people deserve.

9. Samuel Scheffler, *Boundaries and Allegiances* (Oxford University Press, 2001).

10. Op. cit., 191.

11. Ronald Dworkin, *Law's Empire* (Cambridge, MA: Harvard University Press, 1986), p. 206; See also his *Sovereign Virtue: The Theory and Practice of Equality* (Cambridge, MA: Harvard University Press, 1986).

12. Amartya Sen, *Inequality Reexamined* (Cambridge, MA: Harvard University Press, 1992).

CHAPTER 5

Complex Justice

Aging quarterbacks are not like wine. They do not get better with age.
(Mike Freeman on the benching of Quarterback Vinny Testaverde,
New York Times, October 1, 2002)

All [the canons of justice] suffer the aristocratic fault of hyperexclusiveness . . . To correct this failing requires going from a claim establishment that is monistic and homogeneous to one that is pluralistic and heterogeneous.

(Nicholas Rescher)

What is just often seems context-sensitive, depending on the particular rules governing the institution in question. A nonvicious relativism prevails, so that what is appropriate in one domain is not so in another. We pay factory workers by the hour, but salespersons by commission and building contractors by the amount agreed upon in advance. In sit-down restaurants we pay for our food after we receive our meals, but in fast-food restaurants we pay before we receive our food. We pay one standard fare for a ride on the New York City subway regardless of distance traveled, but we pay according to distance when riding the London underground or the Washington, D.C. Metro. A salesperson working on a commission who makes 40% of his company's sales has a clear claim to 40% of the funds set aside for commissions, but a political candidate who loses an election by a 40:60 ratio does not have a legitimate claim to occupy the office 40% of the time. He has no right to occupy it at all. In the Supreme Court of the land, clerks write briefs for the Justices, which would be considered plagiarism in an academic setting. Similarly, anonymous speech writing is permitted and even applauded in politics, whereas students could face expulsion for having another person write their speeches, term papers, or dissertations. What is considered immoral cheating when students or academic teachers engage in it is permitted when politicians, generals, and Supreme Court Justices engage in it. The American Medical Association code of ethics prohibits breaches of confidentiality by a physician except as the law requires, for gunshot wounds and contagious diseases, but the British Medical Association code of conduct leaves the matter up to the individual discretion of the doctor in relation to his or her patient, whereas the World Medical Association treats confidentiality as an absolute duty. A 35% average is excellent for a batter in baseball but disastrous for an airplane pilot.

Samuel Scheffler observes such plurality against monolithic egalitarians who would reject resource differences where talent or ability is involved but not where choice has created a difference.

If I have a less successful career as a philosopher than you do because your superior philosophical gifts enable you to refute all my arguments, then, contrary to what the generalized claim [about equality] might lead us to expect, most people would not regard that as unfair. Nor would most think it unfair if a naturally gifted professional athlete were offered a more lucrative contract than his less talented teammate. On the other hand, most people would consider it outrageous if an emergency room doctor left an injured patient untreated simply because the patient's injury resulted from a foolish but voluntary decision. And few would think it acceptable to deny legal counsel to an indigent defendant on the ground that her inability to pay for an attorney was the result of poor financial decision making on her part.[1]

There seem to be several spheres of justice, each with its own internal logic. In his book *Spheres of Justice*, Michael Walzer has set forth a theory of complex justice.[2] Instead of one fundamental principle, he argues for a radical plurality of concepts, with a kind of "complex equality" playing a special role. According to Walzer, considerations of justice always occur within a bounded political community, wherein members create their own social goods. Each of these social goods determines a peculiar criterion of just distribution. In the case of the institution of money, the criterion of distribution is the free market; in the case of health care, the distributive criterion is need; in the case of distributing jobs and entrance into higher education, the relevant criterion is merit; in the case of democratic citizenship, it is equality before the law. Walzer's approach is bottom-up: the criteria of justice arise from the shared meanings that individuals in the community give to their social institutions, rather than being top-down, descending from some abstract theory. Since each sphere has an autonomy of its own, a type of complex equality develops, with an evening out of benefits. The financier may be superior at money-making but poor at science, writing literature, and sports. The end result is that tyranny via dominance is obviated. "Dominance describes a way of using social goods that isn't limited by their intrinsic meaning or that shapes those meanings in its own sphere" (*Spheres*, 10f). My main departure from Walzer's program concerns his tendency toward moral relativism. He writes, "Justice is relative to social meanings. Indeed, the relativity of justice follows from the classic non-relative definition, giving each person his due, as much as it does from my own proposal, distributing goods for 'internal' reasons. . . . There are no external or universal principles that can replace [local accounts of justice]."[3]

In contrast to Walzer, a nonrelative, objectivist perspective that incorporates pluralism appeals to an external set of principles to constrain interpretations of justice, a core morality, including a concept of natural desert (discussed in Chapter 2), serving as a transcendental sphere that interpenetrates every other sphere. By Walzer's criterion, a society would be justified in disenfranchising or even enslaving a minority, such as the case of Seba (see Chapter 1) or endorsing brutal rituals such as clitoridectomies (as some African tribes still do), or discriminating against people on the basis of gender, religion, or sexual preference. An objectivist rejects such implications, holding to the view that some moral principles apply universally, so that a rational externalist assessment of a culture is possible. Abridging liberty without a stringent moral reason, as in the case of slavery, is morally wrong, as is causing unnecessary suffering, such as occurs in the practice of clitoridectomies, female genital mutilation. In addition, contra Walzer's communitarian nationalism, justice has application beyond local borders; there is a universal, global application of justice.[4] On the objectivist account, justice arises from social meanings but is constrained by core moral principles, such as refraining from injury, promise keeping, and natural desert (see Chapters 2 and 6). This is not to deny some internalist assessment of morality. Positive morality involves social acceptance. It may begin with cultural approval, but it doesn't end there, for we may assess the culture itself from a meta-level rational perspective. Formally, we can say, "Some act A is a justice-related duty in sphere S for society T if society T understands that duty to be one arising from within sphere S." But it is a prima facie duty, which may be overridden by a more stringent universal duty, such as giving people what they morally deserve. Unlike Walzer's account, the objectivist account recognizes a two-way street between abstract principles and the spheres of justice. Reflective equilibrium operates between our moral principles and our institutions, so that the principles may prescribe changes in the institutions, but the experience within our institutions may prescribe revision of our moral principles.

To sum up, Walzer's pluralistic bottom-up theory of justice is partly true and a good place to begin a study of justice. People do create society and social institutions (though some institutions measure up better to moral principles than others), and these institutions have an internal set of criteria to govern the distribution of goods within their borders. But some moral principles apply universally and cut across every sphere of justice.

Justice is one important social virtue among others, including liberty and utility. Justice deals with the proper criteria for distributing benefits and burdens among individuals within a society, primarily a bounded society, but spreading out to the human society at large. However, justice does need a central agency to decide on the criteria for allocating benefits and burdens, as well as to execute the distributive process, make laws, enforce contracts, tax surplus wealth, and redistribute it. It brings to court, tries, convicts, and punishes malfeasors. Social life is complex, made up of several spheres or areas of social interaction, each with an internal coherent set of norms. The rules governing the free market are different from those governing a health care system or a university system or the game of baseball.

The question arises at the outset, Are the descriptions of justice within diverse spheres meant to be descriptive or prescriptive? The answer is both. There is a sense in which any social institution that has survived over time has a presumption in its favor. Unless we can point to reasons why we should abandon it, we ought to accept it, reforming it where our moral principles or social contingencies require us to do so. Forms of life are experiments in living. Some experiments are confirmed better than others, and others like slavery in ancient Greece and eighteenth-century Europe and America or communism in the former Soviet Union should be abandoned because of moral and/or prudential reasons. Hopefully, slavery and war will someday fit into this category of outmoded institutions.

The plurality approach to justice is analogous to other axiological concepts, such as *good* or *fitting*. Although *good* may signify the most general term of commendation, it is applied differently in different contexts. We may call such concepts *functional terms*, since they don't name things, but designate processes whereby criteria are satisfied. A good car meets different criteria from a good building, a good army officer from a good artist, a good person from good weather, and a good joke from a good argument or theory. To refer back to our opening epigraph, aging quarterbacks, unlike wine, do not get better with age. The applications all have something in common, more than a loose family resemblance, but the nature of the application may be quite radical. Similarly, justice seems to be a functional concept that satisfies different criteria in different forms of life.[5]

In what follows I will identify nine separate spheres of justice: the communal, health care, welfare, citizenship, economic, moral inter-relational, law, appointments and jobs, and war. These spheres seem of special significance, especially for cultures like ours. Although these are the most salient spheres of justice, the list is not exhaustive. These spheres seem especially important in a society like ours. They have evolved over time, as they have developed in a process of meeting fresh contingencies. They will no doubt further evolve. Some of my interpretations of how justice works within a given sphere will seem controversial to some readers. This is to be expected. Much more needs to be said, qualifying each sphere, than I am able to say in this work. I offer my sketch as a panoramic outline of the topic, welcoming challenges and revisions.

Nine Spheres of Justice

Community

The most immediate place where we meet concerns of justice is in close communities such as the family, the religious community, tribe, village, and club. The commune and kibbutz are prominent examples of artificially created communities. In these cooperative networks, love, loyalty, and solidarity are dominant virtues, and need is the principal criterion of justice. Here Marx's dictum "From each according to his ability, to each according to his need" has its coherent place.[6] In such intimate relationships, we are motivated to make sacrifices for those with the most urgent need. Thomas Nagel gives the example of a family with two children, one of whom is highly talented and the other who is severely handicapped. The family has the option of living either in the suburbs where the two adults and the talented child will flourish, and the handicapped child be no worse off, or in the city where the handicapped child will receive special care but the other three will be worse off than if they lived in a suburban home. Nagel argues that in such cases need should trump other values, prompting the family to move to the city.[7] Derek Parfit calls this theory of giving priority to the worst off *Prioratarianism*, contrasting it both with egalitarianism, which treats each member equally, and utility, which seeks to maximize aggregate welfare. It also differs from meritocracy which rewards people according to their merit or desert.[8] Love covers a multitude of sins in close communities, so that desert and merit are minimized as criteria of distribution, replaced by the maxim of "one for all and all for one." If five friends are pushing their car up a hill, once the car is at the apex, where it can be started due to gravitational force, each shares equally in the benefit, even though some may have worked harder or more effectively in pushing the car up the hill. Communitarian justice focuses on solidarity, giving priority to distribution according to need with equality as the default principle.

Some philosophers generalize from the communitarian sphere, seeking to make need and equality the dominant principles in every sphere, the economic, political, and social status spheres, and the moral sphere, where they fit less coherently. Communitarians like Alasdair MacIntyre and Michael Sandel justify patriotism and strong nationalism by appealing to this solidarity criterion, but it seems an instance of misplaced concretion, for the nation is too large an entity—really an abstraction, consisting of institutions and numerous individuals whom we cannot relate to intimately.[9]

To illustrate the limitations of the solidarity criterion, consider the example of pushing the car up the hill. Friends, no doubt, would all help push the vehicle voluntarily. But suppose my car is stalled, and I ask you and four other bystanders to help me push the car up a long hill. You would be within your rights to require a reasonable fee for such service, and depending how much I desired my car to get pushed up the hill, I would probably agree to pay you all the fee. Here economic criteria of exchange of money for service replaces need as the relevant criterion of distribution.

Health Care

Personal health is another sphere of justice where need is the relevant criterion for distribution, for health is a basic need for a minimally decent life. Medicine has an internal goal of curing illness. Not only did medicine originate to cure disease, but its essential function is to treat sickness and restore people to health according to their need.[10] Hence, wealth ought not to be a decisive factor in receiving basic health care.

The criterion of need can sometimes be overridden, say in the case where the patient has been irresponsible. I once heard a cigarette smoker, who smoked a pack of cigarettes a day, insist that if he contracted lung cancer or emphysema as a result of his smoking, he had just as much right to medical benefits as anyone who refrained from smoking but nevertheless contracted lung cancer. But such asseverations abrogate our notion of moral responsibility. Here desert should override need as the relevant criterion, especially when there are scarce medical resources. We might well decide to treat the smoker-cancer patient, especially if we had ample resources, but it would be out of mercy and benevolence, not justice, and he would take a place lower down on the waiting list.[11]

Although a prima facie case can be made for prioritization of health care according to need, sometimes that principle is overridden by the principle of triage. In wartime, military doctors separate the injured into three categories: (1) patients who have acute needs but who will probably die even with treatment; (2) patients who are badly wounded but who with limited medical care can be saved and returned to active duty; and (3) patients who will probably recover through their own recuperative powers with little if any medical care. Under triage, preference is given to group 2, where limited resources can do the most good. Here the utilitarian principle of efficiency is operative. This is not a principle of justice, but it is not unjust to act this way either. Whether a type of triage should be applied to civil society is a debatable issue, but medical ethicists like Daniel Callahan of the Hastings Center have argued that given limited medical resources in the United States, a triage-like policy of rationing should be implemented, spending less on the elderly and terminally ill patients and more on infants and children, where the resources could do more good.[12]

Citizenship

The most comprehensive sphere of justice for a bounded society is citizenship. Representational democracy, such as we know it, with all its liabilities, seems the best or least harmful way to organize a society. As Winston Churchill quipped, it is the worst form of government, except for all the others. With its checks and balances distributed among the various branches of government, representational democracy offers the possibility of self-correcting reform in place of revolution and tyranny. It holds that liberty is a primary value, and it is committed to the protection of minority groups and minority points of view. Freedom of thought, speech, and action are morally defensible values. Equality is also a democratic value. Democracy holds that all citizens are equal before the law and that their interests should be given equal consideration by the governing agency. Citizens are promised an equal vote, equal protection of the law, and equal opportunity to compete for coveted positions. Equal citizenship also means that each citizen has a prima facie obligation to defend his or her county, to be a candidate for conscription in time of war. The idea of democratic citizenship rules out discrimination on the basis of socially irrelevant features, such as race, gender, religion, and sexual preference. But the formal equality of democratic citizenship only promises that each claim will be judged impartially by whatever criteria prevail in a segment of social life. It does not offer equal results, even though equal representation in various areas may be appealing to egalitarians.

Equal citizenship in a society like ours means being guaranteed a minimal basic education: literacy, numeracy, basic science, and basic critical thinking, including moral decision making. The state has a compelling interest in providing basic education, ensuring that its citizens are able to handle the complexities of responsible citizenship in a modern democracy. Sometimes the state's secular orientation may invade the family's value system to such a degree that the family wishes to withdraw their children from the state schools and educate them in contexts more amenable to its values, either at home or in private schools. As long as basic skills and democratic moral values are inculcated, the family should be at liberty to choose its own manner of education. Whether this requires that the state support its freedom through a voucher system or state scholarships is more debatable, and reasonable people can differ on this issue. On the one hand, we ought to ensure a high level of public education where basic educational skills and moral values are effectively taught. On the other hand, parents should be allowed a great deal of latitude in choosing how their children will be educated. If a family wants to use its surplus wealth to educate its children rather than to have a more expensive vacation or lifestyle, there are no apparent grounds for the state to prevent this, even if such enhanced education will result in inequality of academic abilities between the more frugal families and the less educationally committed. The greatest British intellect of the nineteenth century, John Stuart Mill, was home schooled (his father even forbade him from going to Oxford University lest it should stultify his creative brilliance!). On the other hand, long before Mill, the poor Jewish child Hillel placed himself near the skylight on the school roof in order to listen to lessons being taught. He fell asleep and was discovered sleeping in the snow in the morning. He was rewarded by the authorities, who, recognizing his dedication, waived tuition and admitted him as a scholar. Hillel became the leading Talmudic scholar of his day. Brilliance can emerge out of the common people where there is sufficient motivation.

So while the ideal of basic equal citizenship does require a minimum of basic education, it doesn't require that the family be prevented from supplementing that education or that some children excel above others in the learning process. Differences will emerge owing to heredity, family background, the influence of the individual school, teachers, and peers. Equal citizenship in education is compatible with meritocracy.

Some people hold that justice essentially means "equality before the law." But this is an ambiguous concept that may mean either "equal enforcement of the existing laws" or "substantive laws which are not based on arbitrary or unfair discrimination" ("equality in law"). Regarding mere equality before the law or equal protection of the law, John Stuart Mill expressed the fundamental problem:

> The justice of giving equal protection to the rights of all, is maintained by those who support the most outrageous inequality in the rights themselves. Even in slave countries it is theoretically admitted that the rights of the slave, such as they are, ought to be as sacred as those of the master; and that a tribunal which fails to enforce them with equal strictness is wanting in justice.

The principle of equality before the law is no more than one of consistency or nonarbitrariness, a formal principle treating equals equally and unequals unequally, but saying nothing about the substantive criterion for making the relevant judgment.

The U.S. Supreme Court has ruled that gender sometimes constitutes a relevant difference in application of the law. Noting biological differences, in *Schlesinger v. Ballard* it upheld differential tenure rules for male and female naval officers; under these rules women are entitled to a longer period of service before mandatory discharge for want of promotion. Equality before the law may sometimes involve inequality of treatment, especially when that treatment is based on morally relevant considerations. This leads us to make a point about the importance of morality in civic life.

An illustration of treating citizens as equals is the institution of the national draft, exemplified in the Enrollment and Conscription Act of 1863, the first military draft in American history. President Lincoln and his War Department deemed the draft necessary to win the Civil War, so that every able-bodied male was subject to a lottery to determine whether he should be conscripted. But the loophole was that an exemption could be bought for $300. This meant that the rich could purchase exemption from the draft, but the poor could not. As the resentful poor put it, "Does [Lincoln] think that poor men are to give their lives and let the rich men pay $300 in order to stay home?"[13] The principle of equal citizenship is violated when money can determine who should risk his or her life for the nation, and so one can understand the resentment that led to riots in New York City over the Conscription Act.

Ethics

An all-encompassing, interpenetrating sphere of justice must now be briefly noted—the general sphere of morality itself. Within the realm of civic life morality takes on a special role, which enjoins that desert sometimes trump civic equality. As Martin Luther King, Jr. said in his historic 1963 March on Washington "I Have a Dream" speech, people ought to be judged not by "the color of their skin but by the content of their character." We should judge people according to their moral integrity, for morality is the glue that holds a family, a community, a corporation, and a nation together. We rightly honor those who risk their lives for the common good, such as soldiers defending their country, or those who act with uncommon virtue, such as Gandhi or Mother Teresa. We endeavor to tailor our laws to the shape of our morality. We deny the vote to convicted felons. We outlaw discrimination on the basis of race, gender, and religion, but we enjoin discrimination on the basis of excellence, virtue, and selfless service. We seek to distribute positions of trust and responsibilities to those who prove especially honorable and virtuous. Moral virtue is a necessary, though not a sufficient condition, for responsible positions in society. Unless citizens are basically honest and conscientious, a society cannot survive, let alone flourish. We expect the corporate executives of companies like Enron, WorldCom, the Arthur Anderson accounting firm, and the like to be not only competent business people, but also people of integrity, and when they fail, we rightly censor them as betraying the public trust. Although in acting irresponsibly, they may not break an existing law, the harm done to employees, clients, and the public under their watch exceeds that of the common thief who burgles a few homes. Moral virtue is not a separate sphere of justice. It is a sphere without boundaries, a country without borders or walls, which permeates every other sphere. The very flourishing and survival of society depends upon it mixing evenly throughout systems of justice, as when a red dye is added to pure water.[14]

Law

The function of the law is to dispense justice. It does so in two separate ways, through criminal and civil law. The purpose of criminal law is to protect society from harm, both removing the accused from society and, if found guilty, punishing him for his crime. When the threat of immorality becomes especially serious, we create a special sphere, that of criminal law, wherein we prosecute and then punish those found to be guilty of violations of the law. In such trials we first determine guilt and the degree to which the malfeasor deserves punishment. Although we hope that punishment deters future crimes, we do not punish people simply because it will likely deter prospective criminals, but because the actual criminals deserve their punishment. We will examine the concept of criminal justice in Chapter 8.

The purpose of civil law is to resolve conflicts of interest equitably (e.g., settling a will or deciding who has power of attorney) and compensating those wrongfully harmed for damages. If through a physician's neglect, a deformed baby is born, the baby may be due a financial award. Justice in law is Janus faced, looking in two opposite directions: toward the past (the conservative face) and toward the future (its reform face). It has a conservative face looking backwards when it applies existing statutes, as when it applies the law to criminal offenses or traffic violations. Its reform or liberal face is manifest through progressive legislation or judicial review. Examples of reform in law are welfare laws to protect the worst off members of society, minimum wage laws, and laws prohibiting smoking in public places.

Similarly, with judicial review, sometimes the court applies existing statutes to a present case. At other times, natural justice seems to cry out for a new interpretation of an existing principle. The best example of this reform face is the U.S. Supreme Court's decision in *Brown v. Board of Education* (1954) when it ruled against the legitimacy of segregationist school districts in Topeka, Kansas, overturning a previous Supreme Court decision, *Plessey v. Ferguson* (1896), which had stood for fifty-eight years. The Court ruled in *Brown* that the doctrine of "separate but equal" espoused in *Plessey* violated the equal protection clause of the Fourteenth Amendment. Surely, those who drew up the Fourteenth Amendment didn't have the prohibition of racial segregation in mind when they wrote this amendment into the Constitution. The decision to outlaw racial segregation was based on our nation's growing understanding of the moral rights of citizens to enjoy the full benefits of society together with the realization that segregation would tend to enhance the power of the more powerful groups in society. Note that at this time the policy in Israel is segregation of Jews from Palestinians: a physical wall is actually being built between the two communities. One could defend the Israeli segregationist policy as just, if one focuses on the conservative face of the law in its function to protect its citizens from each other. The Supreme Court decision in *Brown* focused on its reform face.

The conservative face of justice looks toward desert or merit as the proper criterion to be applied to situations, whereas the reform face looks toward need or equality (or the reduction of inequality) as the appropriate criterion of assessment. Both have a place in the Janus-faced repertoire of justice.[15]

The point of distinguishing between criminal and civil law and between the conservative and reform faces of the law is to show the different manifestations and meanings of justice depending on the social context.

Welfare

Welfare and unemployment benefits in an affluent society like ours constitute a separate sphere of justice wherein a combination of need and desert are the relevant criteria of distribution. Need itself creates a prima facie duty on the part of the society to help those who are worse off, but if they are undeserving, perhaps free loaders or even criminals, the duty to support them with the tax dollars of the productive members of society may be partly overridden. On the other hand, those who make special efforts to become self-sufficient, the *deserving poor* (to use a phrase that has unfortunately gone out of fashion), deserve to helped more than those who fail to try to improve their lots or waste the opportunities they have been given.

Similarly, assigning positions of status and important jobs and leadership positions to people is within the sphere of justice in which merit is the dominant criterion. We would be irresponsible to hire anyone but the best qualified surgeon to operate on patients or to appoint anyone but the best qualified army officer to lead troops into a dangerous battle.[16]

Economics

We turn next to the economic sphere where society has created a specific institutional activity, the free-market system. Capitalism fits Walzer's theory of a human creation that has a logic of its own. We could have other types of economic systems, say, barter or a command economy, but at this time and place in history there are utilitarian grounds for preferring capitalism. It is the most efficient system we know of for producing aggregate wealth, creating markets, and satisfying wants and needs. The values of the sphere of the market are liberty, ability (merit), and luck. Even desert enters into the picture within the workplace, as we normally think that if one person works harder than others, he should get paid more. The one criterion the market does not respect is equality. Because money, goods, and services can be freely traded, inequalities will inevitably emerge. Of course, we could choose a command or socialist economy, in which case we would get more equality but less wealth. The saying that "a rising tide lifts all boats" applies to the free market.

Capitalism is almost too good to be true. It enjoins selfish (or, to put it more mildly, self-interested) behavior, promising that an Invisible Hand will ultimately cause such a procedure to redound to the common good. Although capitalism in general serves a utilitarian purpose, utilitarianism itself via the principle of Diminishing Marginal Utility (which holds that a unit of resource creates more welfare as it is redistributed from the rich person's surplus wealth to the poor man's purse) urges us to constrain capitalism and institute a system of taxation to make better use of surplus wealth, redistributing it from the wealthy to the poor. It might be better to say that the free-market system is not unjust but can be justified by utilitarian principles, which in turn direct us to mitigate the extremes of wealth and poverty produced by capitalism.

Money should be strictly confined to its own sphere of property and commodities. Wealth may legitimately govern how large and nice one's house is, what kind of art one owns, or, within limits, what kind of car one drives. But some things ought not to be subject to wealth. Political offices, power, and influence are outside the proper sphere of wealth. Criminal justice must not be for sale, nor should one be allowed to purchase criminal services, such as hiring someone to maim or murder your enemy. Love, marriage, and friendship ought not to be bought. Prizes and honors, such as a Hollywood Oscar, the Medal of Honor, or the Most Valuable Player Award in a sport should not be subject to financial power.[17]

But the wider social good has a claim on entrepreneurial success and individual wealth, so that progressive taxation may be justified to redistribute some surplus wealth to where it is needed most.

Libertarians hold that taxation is unjust because it robs the entrepreneur of his deserved assets. Robert Nozick has argued, "Taxation of earnings from labor is on a par with forced labor."[18] But this seems to overlook important elements about justice.

Morality focuses primarily on individuals. Groups have no essential reality; they don't feel pain or pleasure, happiness or unhappiness, though they can succeed and fail. They don't have personal identity. They are not persons, but legal fictions; they are simply composites of individuals.

Both communitarians and Rawlsians may be mistaken in underemphasizing individuality and overemphasizing the community. Rawls says, "We see then that the *difference principle* represents, in effect, an agreement to regard the distribution of natural talents as a common asset and to share in the benefits of this distribution whatever it turns out to be."[19] But this is mistaken. The individual owns his or her talents, whether they be intelligence, athletic prowess, artistic ability, or beauty. We have a responsibility to use our talents as good stewards for the good of the community and world, but we are allowed to do so in our own way. Being autonomous agents, we don't belong to the state, nor do our talents belong to the society, any more than our bodies belong to the state or community. To accept otherwise is to endorse slavery.

Our notion of liberty requires that we be permitted to develop our talents in a manner each of us sees fit. Kant's notion of an *imperfect duty* is applicable here. We have a duty to develop our talents, but which talents we develop and to what extent we develop them is up to us. We are granted a large measure of freedom, though it also follows that in the words of the Bible, "Every one to whom much is given, of him much will be required" (Luke 12:48b). Conversely, to whom little is given, little is to be required.

Yet individuals do live in communities, in families, in social groupings, in villages, towns, cities, and states, a point ignored by libertarians such as John Hospers and Nozick. We are, to quote Aristotle, "political animals." As such, we have a duty to promote the social good. Because of an exaggerated focus on personal liberty, libertarians like Nozick argue that people are entitled to all of their earnings, so that taxation is a form of forced labor. We examined this theory of justice in Chapter 3 and argued for its limited validity, maintaining that it omitted salient features of interdependent social existence. He agreed that basketball fans had a right to pay Wilt Chamberlain extra money to watch him play and that Chamberlain is entitled to his income, since this entitlement flows from appropriate legal conditions. But just because Chamberlain is entitled to receive the extra funds in no way entails that he has a right to keep all of that money.

Rawls put the rebuttal to Nozick this way:

> Taxes and restrictions are all in principle foreseeable, and holdings are acquired on the known condition that certain corrections will be made. The objection that the difference principle enjoins continuous and capricious interference with private transactions is based on a misunderstanding.[20]

Because it assumes an erroneous atomistic view of human nature, libertarianism, such as is evinced in Nozick's argument comparing taxation with forced labor, is a false theory. The truth is, in the words of the poet John Donne, "No man is an island, entire of itself." Mammals live in groups, and this is especially true of human beings. We are nurtured by mothers, reared and socialized in families by parents and siblings and relatives. We are taught a language and a set of customs. We are educated into a culture, internalizing a tradition of myths, symbols, and history. We acquire social and academic skills that enable us to navigate through the labyrinthine maze of a complex, interpersonal world. In a sense, human beings are not born; rather, they are constructed by their environment, especially their families and communities. Since we are all in each other's debt, we have some responsibility to come to the aid of those who are badly off through no fault of their own. Giving back to the community should be seen as an expression of gratitude for the benefits of community and civilization and an acknowledgment that some of us are more fortunate than others. It seems that capitalism needs to be constrained by a progressive tax system in order to diminish the gap between the rich and poor and to approximate equal opportunity (see Chapter 4).

The Sphere of Positions

In the realm of hiring people for jobs and positions of special responsibility, a hiring or promotion committee ideally consists of experts in their field, who are able to judge candidates impartially, according to standards of merit. Here the salient value is Utility Maximization or Efficiency. What is Efficiency?

Efficiency is the ratio between input and output. The more output for a given input the better. For an illustration consider a mechanical device and take gasoline-powered cars. The input is gallons of gas; the output is miles traveled. In an inefficient engine some fuel is expended merely in heating the engine rather than in driving pistons. This impedes the operation of the engine, for it requires using still more energy to counteract the unfortunate effects of the heating. Fuel burned with those effects is wasted. Similarly, a more Pareto-efficient society will be one in which people do better in relation to their expenditures of time and effort in trying to achieve their goals. When some, whether interfering individuals (e.g., criminals or harassers) or the state impede others in achieving their goals, we must employ still other people to impede the impeders, spending time and energy in a manner not productive—negating the negaters. The analogy is applicable to society in at least two ways. On the one hand, it instructs us to leave people alone, leaving them to attain their goals in their own way. Government should not impede their morally acceptable endeavors. It should not become the overheated engine, burning up fuel needed for the proper functioning of the machine itself. On the other hand, it instructs us to hire the best people for each job. Discrimination on the basis of race or gender is inefficient, but discrimination on the basis of ability is not. We want the best surgeons to perform our open-heart surgery, the best airplane pilots to fly our planes, the best generals to lead our armies. This is why strong affirmative action is unjust. It violates the inner logic of appointments to positions of responsibility that prescribes merit as the criterion and employs one of irrelevance to the job itself, race, ethnicity, or gender. Our Constitution (especially the Fourteenth Amendment) proclaims "equal protection of the laws," which has meant that all irrelevant discrimination is a violation of our equal rights as citizens. So reverse racism, though not as bad as the original racism, is against justice in the spheres of citizenship and appointments. It should be illegal. In Western society and wherever efficiency has become a salient value, a tradition of impartial review has grown up in hiring and promoting people in any large corporation, whether it be the military, a business, a university, or an athletic team. The system must be fair and objective. Vice Admiral James Stockdale describes the Navy selection board proceedings as follows:

> The first order of business is to stand, raise your right hand, put your left hand on the Bible, and swear to make the best judgment you can, on the basis of merit, without prejudice. You're sworn to confidentiality regarding all board members' remarks during the proceedings. Board members are chosen on their experience and understanding; they often have knowledge of the particular individuals under consideration. They must feel free to speak their minds. They read and grade dozens of dossiers, and each candidate is discussed extensively. At voting time, a member casts his vote by selecting and pushing a "percent confidence" button, visible only to himself, on a console attached to his chair. When the last member pushes the button, a totalizer displays the numerical average "confidence" of the board. No one knows who voted what.[21] In any hierarchy where people's fates are at stake it is important that the most competent people are chosen for the job.

Just War

Finally, we need to say a few things about justice in war. Justice in war is based on the natural right of self-defense, systematically set forth in Just War Theory, a set of principles that were developed by St. Augustine (354–430), Thomas Aquinas

(1225–1274), and Hugo Grotius (1583–1645) among others. Although many versions of Just War Theory exist, they all regard going to war (*jus ad bellum*), at best, as a necessary evil, justified by the right of self-defense, entered into only as a last resort, when peace is not a viable option, and when the prospects of going to war promise a reasonable expectation of the benefits involved exceeding the costs. Just War Theory further prescribes rules for engaging in justified conflict (*jus in bello*):

Proportionality: No more force must be exerted than is necessary to accomplish the task of winning the war.

Discrimination: Violence may only be directed against combatants and their material (e.g., weapons factories and supply lines). Noncombatants may not be intentionally targeted, and prisoners, no longer a viable threat, must be treated with the dignity that is appropriate to every innocent human being.

Just War Theory is not absolutistic. In *supreme emergency*, when the offending side threatens to win the war or impute enormous damage, the violated nation may resort to extraordinary force to save itself. In some situations, Just War Theory may be subject to different interpretations, and so yield up different recommended courses of action. An example would be the dropping of the atom bombs on Hiroshima and Nagasaki in August 1945, bringing an end to the war in the Pacific. On the one hand, contrary to *jus in bello* principles, noncombatants were directly targeted. On the other hand, it was an extreme situation, the alternative being a costly invasion of the Japanese mainland with the prospect of over a million more casualties. The justification for dropping the bombs seems to be utilitarian rather than one of justice, but the act may not have been unjust either. The fact that the United States, under the adroit leadership of General Douglas MacArthur, immediately worked to restore peace and build a viable democracy in Japan, expressed the deepest spirit of justice in war by renouncing vengeance and reestablishing good relations.

The evils of killing and destroying, intrinsic to war, must be used only in extreme situations where the consequences of not going to war would be an even greater evil. Justice in war is *sui generis*, of a unique type, but based on the right of self-defense and the defense of innocent people. Just as a victim has the right to defend himself against a criminal who assaults him, a nation has the right to defend itself against another aggressive nation or terrorist group that assaults it or is about to assault it.

Immediately the question arises: When two or more different spheres that have different conceptions of justice come into contact with one another, what moral principles or requirements should one adhere to in order to establish priority?

This is a difficult question that needs a lot of work, but, as a first attempt to answer it, let me say the following: My moral theory permits a broad latitude of permissible responses, subject to negotiation between interested parties. Whatever is not clearly immoral is permissible, so that the burden of proof generally lies on the person who would restrict your behavior. If no redline principle forbids your action, it is allowed. Of course, we have well-worked-out traditions to guide us in many places. A parent generally has a fundamental duty to his or her family that overrides duties to the wider community or state, except where criminality and the defense of the community and state are concerned. These resolutions strike one as broadly utilitarian. Indeed, most of our morality and political arrangements are broadly utilitarian (Rule—utilitarianism—consisting in practices that have proven themselves over time, but that are always subject to revision).

Let us now bring our results together.

Conclusion

Justice does have a functional aspect, so that it is context dependent. Walzer, in developing the most comprehensive defense of complex justice, is right about there being separate, but interlocking, spheres of justice, each with its own logic and criteria of distribution, but his tendency to relativism needs to be corrected. Some criteria, such as a core of morality, desert, and merit, are universal values that ought to serve as criteria for the distribution of goods, and in the case of negative desert, punishment, in any culture. A communitarian realm exists wherein the dominant criterion of distribution is need. A general citizenship sphere exists wherein the dominant criterion is formal equality, especially equality before the law, an equal obligation to defend one's nation as well as the right to a basic education sufficient for responsible citizenship. It promises each citizen an equal consideration of interests. In the sphere of law, two separate criteria are manifest: a conservative focus on merit and a reforming focus on need and equality. In the social sphere of health care, need is the dominant criterion, but desert is also relevant. In the sphere of awarding places of responsibility and leadership, merit is the relevant criterion. In the sphere of the free market, liberty should be the dominant value, mitigated by the principle of Diminishing Marginal Utility, which would justify imposing a progressive income tax in order to redistribute surplus wealth from the rich to the poor. Underlying all of these spheres is the criterion of moral desert, which qualifies and sometimes overrides the other criteria but has a special application to the sphere of criminal justice. Even in Just War Theory, the offending nation must *deserve* to be attacked and the nation that has been attacked must be sufficiently just to *deserve* being defended.

Injustice occurs when the appropriate criterion of justice is ignored or replaced by another criterion from a different sphere, for example, when wealth, appropriate to economics, invades the political sphere wherein merit should be the relevant criterion.

Conflicts in our ideas may arise when we disagree over the nature of the relevant sphere in which a case arises. Suppose there is a job opening in my company. We would normally think that the job should go to the applicant who is best qualified to fill it, based on impartial review of the credentials. But suppose I own the small business and for the solidarity of my family I want to hire my nephew who desperately needs work. Am I unjust if I hire my nephew rather than a more qualified person? It probably depends on how we characterize the job. Do we exempt small family businesses from the usual meritocratic constraints? It is in cases where legitimate conflict arises over the nature of the relevant sphere of justice that the need for the moral sphere becomes most apparent. Exactly how the override comes about will differ according to the nature of the moral theory involved, but common-sense morality endorses general principles of truthfulness, impartiality, and fidelity over deception, partiality, and infidelity.

I have argued for an objectivist version pluralist theory of justice with different spheres wherein different criteria apply. Injustice occurs both when, within a sphere of justice, the appropriate criterion fails to be observed and when an improper criterion, relevant to another sphere, is observed. For example, when equality, especially equal result, is imported from the sphere of general citizenship into the sphere of positions and jobs, injustice occurs. This is the case with strong affirmative action where people are hired for jobs and appointments to offices according to the principle of equality (or equal results) rather than merit. Money or wealth is proper for the economic sphere, but it should not buy jobs, status, or political power. When wealth becomes the criterion whereby elected officials are chosen, we have a type of inequality, simony, or plutocracy, wherein not merit but money becomes the dominant form of political governance. Similarly, injustice occurs in nepotism, when a public position is treated not according to merit but need, and one is hired because of a solidarity relationship. Injustice also occurs when a criterion other than equality is used in the case of a citizen's status before the law when, for example, status or wealth enter in to determine the outcome.

A fuller defense of complex justice would involve a consequentialist strategy in tying the various spheres together, showing how the inner dynamics of each sphere work together with those of other spheres in producing a total situation of utility or the maximizing of values. Whether a consequentialist interpretation or a nonconsequentialist one is the best interpretation of complex justice is a difficult question that is beyond the scope of this study. But the idea of complex, pluralist justice, combining a bottom-up situational account with an objectivist core morality, constitutes one of the most exciting and formidable challenges of political philosophy.

Notes

1. Samuel Scheffler, "What Is Egalitarianism?" *Philosophy & Public Affairs* 31:1 (2003).

2. Michael Walzer, *Spheres of Justice* (New York: Basic Books, 1983). A good set of critical articles on Walzer's theory is found in David Miller and Michael Walzer, eds., *Pluralism, Justice and Equality* (New York: Oxford University Press, 1995). David Miller's book, *The Principles of Social Justice* (Cambridge, MA: Harvard University Press, 1999), has also been of benefit. The original pluralist approach was delineated by Nicholas Rescher in his book, *Distributive Justice* (Bobbs-Merrill, 1966). See also his *Fairness* (Transaction Press, 2002). My analysis is indebted to all of these works, though it differs from each.

3. *Spheres of Justice*, p. 312. Walzer writes in an e-mail (August 30, 2002) that he doesn't accept moral relativism. But his theory of complex justice seems to move in that direction. I believe Walzer and his *Just and Unjust War* could not have been written by a relativist, but

Walzer's bottom-up, forms of life approach to political philosophy in *Spheres of Justice* needs correcting.

4. I will argue for this in Chapter 6.

5. Similarly, what is fitting depends on its context. Different-sized hats fit different-sized heads, and fitting etiquette or aesthetics depend on the specific situation.

6. The statement was first stated by Marx's predecessor Louis Blanc, but the idea is found as far back at the New Testament, Acts 2:24, where the early Christians pooled their resources for the commonweal.

7. Thomas Nagel, "Equality" in *Mortal Questions* (New York City: Cambridge University Press, 1979).

8. Derek Parfit, "Equality or Priority" delivered as the Lindley lecture at the University of Kansas, November 1991.

9. See Michael Sandel, *Liberalism and the Limits of Justice* (New York City: Cambridge University Press, 1982) and Alasdair MacIntyre, *After Virtue* (South Bend, IN: University of Notre Dame Press, 1981). In *After MacIntyre*, eds. Horton and Mendus (1994), MacIntyre strongly disassociates himself from communitarianism, but this seems to be a change of mind.

10. Bernard Williams put the thesis this way: "Leaving aside preventive medicine, the proper ground of distribution of medical care is ill health; this is a necessary truth. Now in very many societies, while ill health may work as a necessary condition of receiving treatment, it does not work as a sufficient condition, since such treatment costs money, and not all who are ill have the money; hence the possession of sufficient money becomes in fact an additional necessary condition of actually receiving treatment. . . . When we have the situation in which, for instance, wealth is a further necessary condition of the receipt of medical treatment, we can once more apply the notions of equality and inequality; not now in connection with the inequality between the well and the ill, but in connection with the inequality between the rich ill and the poor ill, since we have straightforwardly the situation of those whose needs are the same not receiving the same treatment, though the needs are the grounds of the treatment. This is an irrational state of affairs . . . it is a situation in which reasons are insufficiently operative; it is a situation insufficiently controlled by reasons—and hence by reason itself." Bernard Williams, "The Idea of Equality," in *Philosophy, Politics, and Society*, ed. Peter Laslett and W. G. Runciman (London: Basil Blackwell, 1962), p. 121.

11. Stephen Kershnar points out that a physician could decide to distribute medicine according to those who can pay for it, rather than those who need it. We may call him a *schmoctor* instead of a doctor, and by doing so acknowledge that a new institution (or a modification of the one we have) has been created—*schmedicine* instead of medicine. Nozick denies the thesis that there is an internal logic to medicine based on need (*Anarchy, State, and Utopia*, NY: Basic Books, 1974), pp. 233–5, but I fail to find any argument for his case.

12. Daniel Callahan, *Setting Limits: Medical Goals in an Aging Society* (Georgetown University Press, 1987).

13. James McCague, *The Second Rebellion: The Story of the New York City Draft Riots of 1863* (New York, 1968), p. 54. Quoted in Walzer, *Spheres of Justice*, p. 98.

14. In another sense, it is the most important sphere of a social order, determining the life and health of that order.

15. The best discussion of this Janus face aspect of justice is D. D. Raphael, "Conservative and Prosthetic Justice" in *Political Studies* 12 (1964).

16. The mistake of proponents of strong affirmative action is that they tend to treat such positions as a group civil right rather than a zone of merit, where positions ought to be assigned on the basis of performance and qualifications.

17. See Walzer, *Spheres of Justice*, pp. 100–108, for a good discussion of the sphere of money.

18. Robert Nozick, *Anarchy, State and Utopia* (New York: Basic Books, 1973), p. 169. See also John Hospers, *Libertarianism* (Nash Publishing Co., 1971).

19. John Rawls, *A Theory of Justice* (Cambridge, MA: Harvard University Press, 1971).

20. John Rawls, "The Basic Structure of the Subject," *American Philosophical Quarterly* 14 (1977).

21. James Stockdale, "The World of Epictetus" in L. Pojman, ed., *The Moral Life* (New York: Oxford University Press, 2000), p. 508.

Equal Opportunity

> We have also come to this hallowed spot to remind America of the fierce urgency of now. This is no time to engage in the luxury of cooling off or to take the tranquilizing drug of gradualism. Now is the time to rise from the dark and desolate valley of segregation to the sunlit path of racial justice. Now is the time to open the doors of opportunity to all of God's children. Now is the time to lift our nation from the quicksands of racial injustice to the solid rock of brotherhood. . . . I have a dream that my four children will one day live in a nation where they will not be judged by the color of their skin but by the content of their character.
>
> (Martin Luther King, Jr. "I Have a Dream" speech delivered at the March on Washington, August 28, 1963)

The Ideal of Equal Opportunity

In Chapter 2 we raised the possibility that justice involves giving people equal opportunity. We want to analyze this hypothesis further in this chapter. What does equal opportunity mean, and is it a requirement of justice?

Everyone seems to be in favor of equal opportunity. But if this were really so, why would various groups continue to protest that are not afforded equal opportunity? Are some people simply hypocritical or confused? In this chapter we shall attempt to answer this question. On the one hand, no concept symbolizes our vision of the American way of life more complimentarily—one in which everyone, rich and poor, smart and stupid, speedy and slow, prodigy and late bloomer, is offered an equal chance to succeed in life. Abraham Lincoln, Horatio Alger, Henry Ford, Michael Jordan, Lee Iacocca, and a hundred other rags to riches stories or, if not to riches, to the hall of fame, all confirm this romantic vision of America as a land of equal opportunity. University letterheads proudly announce that they are "equal opportunity employers," and business corporations boast that they believe in "equal opportunity for all."

In the 1950s and 1960s, the civil rights movement summed up its struggle in the phrase "equal opportunity for all." The goal of ending Jim Crow laws in the South and prejudicial practices and institutions throughout America would offer black Americans equal access to the benefits of our nation, including the voting booth, the university, public accommodations, and real estate. In *Brown v. Board of Education* (1954) the U.S. Supreme Court decided that the doctrine of "separate but equal" schools was inherently unequal, for it discriminated unfairly against black children. The drive toward a racially integrated society was launched in the name of equal opportunity. Integration, it was held, would spell the end to injustice, the beginning of a new world order where the children of former slaves would compete on a level playing field with the children of former slave owners. As Martin Luther King, Jr. said in his "I Have a Dream Speech" at the 1963 March on Washington, in this new America people would be judged, not by the color of their skin but by "the content of their character." A true meritocracy in the spirit of universal brotherhood was envisioned. A similar process occurred in the women's movement, opening up new job opportunities for them. Justice became defined as equal opportunity. Implicit in the United Nations' *Declaration on Human Rights* is the principle that every human being in every country and culture should be afforded equal opportunity to a decent life with freedom and dignity.

What is equal opportunity? An examination of the concept of equal opportunity should show that this is not a simple concept, but rather a complex, multifaceted notion, containing paradoxical features, features that may conflict with other values.

The Concept of Equal Opportunity

The concept of equal opportunity is a compound idea, consisting of a noun "opportunity" and an adjective "equal." An opportunity is a chance to get or do something—or, more accurately, a chance for an agent to attain a goal without the hindrance of an obstacle. As such, an opportunity consists of three components: the agent (A) to whom the opportunity (O) belongs; the goal (G) toward which the opportunity is directed; and the absence of a specific obstacle (X), which would otherwise hinder A in attaining G.[1] We can symbolize it this way:

A has an O to reach G just in case no X stands in A's way.

Note the emphasis on the agent as an individual. It is not groups but people as individuals who should have opportunities. Groups do not have rights or personalities; they do not have souls or feel pain or pleasure, though as collections of individuals, we use the term to cover sets of individuals. It follows from the thesis that justice has to do with distributing goods to individuals, for the individual is the appropriate unit of value—not the group or society as a whole.

When we say that two people are equal in something, we mean that they have each been measured by a common standard and the comparison shows that they are equal in the relevant manner. So applying this to the concept of equal opportunity, we may say that two people A and B have an equal opportunity to attain some goal or good (G) with regard to some specific obstacle X, if and only if neither is hindered from attaining G by X. For example, in eliminating the Jim Crow laws which enforced segregation in the United States, the U.S. Supreme Court removed an obstacle preventing blacks from attending many universities in the South. Relative to the obstacle of race, blacks now had equal opportunity to attend the University of Mississippi and the University of Alabama. However, obstacles such as inferior educational backgrounds, study habits, or native intelligence were not removed.

No one can have an equal opportunity with everyone else in every way to attain a goal, for there are obstacles of time and place and personal abilities that deeply distinguish us from each other. As John Schaar notes,

> [N]ot all talents can be developed equally in any given society. Out of the great variety of human resources available to it, a given society will admire and reward some abilities more than others. Every society has a set of values, and these arranged in a more or less tidy hierarchy. These systems of evaluation vary from society to society: Soldierly qualities and virtues were highly admired and rewarded in Sparta, while poets languished. Hence, to be accurate, the equality of opportunity formula must be revised to read: equality of opportunity for all to develop those talents which are highly valued by a given people at a given time.[2]

In our society being a highly skilled surgeon, computer programmer, or basketball player will be rewarded more than being a highly skilled organist, farmer, blacksmith, or teacher. Talents such as being the best drug dealer, thief, con artist, or murderer in the community are positively discouraged.

The doctrine of equal opportunity implies a meritocracy, the practice of appointing the best qualified person for the position in question. Having an equal opportunity to a good implies that irrelevant traits will be excluded from the set of criteria to be used for the assessment. Skin and eye color are irrelevant for college admittance, but grade point average and SAT score are not. Gender is irrelevant for admittance for treatment in a hospital Emergency Room but not for admittance to the Maternity Ward.

The doctrine of equal opportunity, in its fundamental sense, is consistent with unequal results. People are very different from each other in abilities and in effort. Equal opportunity allows competition to sort out those with more talent from those with less and reward the most talented with the goods relevant to those talents. Competition is seen as a good thing, useful in challenging us to develop our potential to the fullest. It assures that we will be treated fairly, according to our achievement, not according to our prior racial or social station. William Galston argues that this vision of equal opportunity constitutes a partial definition of a good society:

> In such a society, the range of social possibilities will equal the range of human possibilities. Each worthy capacity, that is, will find a place within it. No one will be compelled to flee elsewhere in search of opportunities for development, the way ambitious young people had to flee farms and small towns in nineteenth-century societies. Further, each worthy capacity will be treated fairly in the allocation of resources available for individual development within that society.[3]

Equal opportunity assures us of a fair chance to compete for the good things of life.

Types of Equal Opportunity

There are at least four different types of equal opportunity.

a. Arbitrary Equal Opportunity: The Natural Lottery.
b. Meritocratic Equal Opportunity: Napoleonic careers open to talent: Meritocracy.
c. Procedural Equal Opportunity: Each person is free (has the chance) to develop his or her talents. The state may help in providing universal education, welfare, and job training. This is the "toolbox" model of equal opportunity. Give everyone the same tools and let them compete in the marketplace. It will result in unequal results, however.
d. Result-oriented Equal Opportunity: This aims at equal results. We cannot have equal opportunity until everyone is equally talented and equally equipped— that is, has a similar toolbox. The proof of equal opportunity will be equal representation of every ethnic (gender) group in every socially prized sphere.

Let us illustrate these four types of equal opportunity.

Arbitrary Equal Opportunity

In Jorge Luis Borges's "The Lottery of Babylon," we have an illustration of what an arbitrary lottery would look like:

> Like all men in Babylon, I have been proconsul; like all, a slave. I have also known omnipotence, opprobrium, imprisonment. Look: the index finger on my right hand is missing. Look: through the rip in my cape you can see a vermilion tattoo on my stomach. It is the second symbol, Beth. This letter, on nights when the moon is full, gives me power over men whose mark is Gimmel, but it subordinates me to the men of Aleph, who on moonless nights owe obedience to those marked with Gimmel. . . .
>
> I owe this almost atrocious variety to an institution which other republics do not know or which operates in them in an imperfect and secret manner: the lottery. I have not looked into its history; I know that the wise men cannot agree. I know of its powerful purposes what a man who is not versed in astrology can know about the moon. I come from a dizzy land where the lottery is the basis of reality.[4]

Once initiated into a special order, every free man participated in the sacred lottery, which "took place in the labyrinths of the god every sixty nights." The results of the drawing were unpredictable. A lucky draw could bring about one's promotion to the council of wise men or the imprisonment of an enemy or the surprise visit of a beautiful woman in his room. A bad play could bring mutilation, various kinds of infamy, death.

Every aspect of life was affected by this intensification of chance, this "periodical infusion of chaos in the cosmos." It was a type of equality, since no one had any right to expect any more from life than anyone else. The lottery decided all—equally.

But this idea can be applied to (or be seen as a subclass of) prospect-regarding equal opportunity, which Douglas Rae tells us "consists of practices under which the prospects of success are equal for all; . . . nothing about the people affects the result." Examples are lotteries, drawing of lots, or flipping of coins.[5]

Life itself is filled with arbitrary features. There is a natural lottery that determines our genetic makeup, our race and gender, our family origins, the country we are born into, which determines our life chances. Simply being born a human being and not some other animal or a plant is a feature of this natural lottery. We accept the natural lottery as a given, but part of equal opportunity, as applied to human beings, is to offset some of the unequal features of arbitrary processes and allow other forms of equal opportunity to function.

Meritocratic Equal Opportunity

In the 1790s, Napoleon Bonaparte rose rapidly through the ranks of the French Army and, as general, broke from the tradition of appointing officers from the nobility and opened the field to anyone with the requisite talents, knowing from his own experience that a policy of careers open to talent would produce a more effective fighting force. Impartial meritarian criteria should be used in the choice of candidates to fill positions. It doesn't matter whether you come from a wealthy or poor family, had a private or public school education, or belong to the upper or lower class. All that we care about is whether you're the best qualified for the job. If Michael Jordan's skin had green polka dots and he was illiterate, he would still have been the most sought-after player in basketball.

Meritocratic equal opportunity hopefully will lead to a convergence of the natural and the social aristocracies. Its justifications are efficiency, the fulfilling of social promises and expectations, respecting the individual for his or her talents, and the intrinsic connection between practices and qualifications.

Pure Procedural Equal Opportunity

Each person is free (has the chance) to develop his or her talents. The state may help in providing universal education, welfare, and job training. It offers each citizen a similar "toolbox," which allows him or her to compete in the marketplace. But equal input of resources produces unequal prospects of success. As Jennifer Hochschild puts it:

> Activities ranging from a poker game to a high school education are examples of means-regarding equal opportunity. Everyone abides by the same rules (a full house beats 3 of a kind, grades of D or better lead to promotion); everyone

is given the same means (7 cards; free compulsory school attendance). The purpose of the activity is to distinguish winners from losers in ways that people deem fair because the outcome reflects relevant characteristics of the actors.[6]

On this model, providing means-regarding equal opportunity in a racial context requires more than abolishing de jure segregation and second-class citizenship. It calls for providing equal means, not just identical rules, to blacks and whites. At a minimum, schools must be desegregated and/or improved so that black children have the same academic experience as white children; employers must pay the same wages and grant similar promotions to equally qualified blacks and whites; cities must be redistricted so that the electoral arithmetic favors black candidates in some places as much as white candidates in others.

The toolbox metaphor refers to the external means a contestant is given by society. But contestants also need a set of skills, internal means. Society can give the external means to people without changing their personality or character, but the internal qualities do cause such changes.[7]

External means, such as better schools, improved job prospects, and redistricting, do favor the prospects of black candidates for positions. But problems arise. What constitutes a better education? Should the state coerce institutions to institute affirmative action programs, admitting blacks with lower scores (lower SAT or GRE scores or, abilities)? Should the state be involved in implementing job decisions? What kind? Is redistricting for purposes of increasing black political power constitutional? And how do we know whether some people decline to use some of these tools? Are unequal results between individuals and groups an indication of prejudice and unjust discrimination, or simply a function of differences in human abilities?

There is a problem in turning children into undifferentiated vessels into which society pours the "right" mix of ingredients to produce identical products. (On this model, if X wants to be a car mechanic or carpenter rather than a lawyer or physician, it is evidence that he hasn't been given equal opportunity in terms of internal means.) Hochschild writes: "When do we declare that all children have an equal enough set of skills so that we may switch from providing equal means to encouraging their remaining differences to distinguish them in accord with the ideal of equal opportunity? As far as I can tell—bottomless swamps to be skirted around rather than plunged into."[8]

John Rawls, rejecting weak equal opportunity, seems to hold something like this version of equal opportunity.

[F]air equality of opportunity . . . must not be confused with the notion of careers open to talents; nor must one forget that since it is tied with the difference principle its consequences are quite distinct from the liberal interpretation of the two principles taken together. In particular I shall try to show . . . that this principle is not subject to the objection that it leads to a meritocratic society.[9]

Rawls wants to separate equal opportunity which promotes talent, while being mitigated by the difference principle, the principle that would share the economic and social benefits accrued by the talented with the worst-off members of society.

Result-Oriented Equal Opportunity

The formula here is:

Equal Opportunity = Equal Results.

Some would go further than moderate equal opportunity and argue that unless and until we have equal group results in all significant life spheres, we have not achieved equal opportunity. Until we have the same average pay for all racial, ethnic, and gender groups and an approximate equality of representation of such in each profession (law, medicine, corporate executives, university professors, physicists, plumbers, electricians—and I guess basketball players and criminals too), we will not have achieved equal opportunity. (e.g., A few years ago the California legislature passed a bill requiring that University of California graduate students in approximate proportion to their ethnic makeup in the population. The governor vetoed the bill.) The Presumption of Equal Results: downsize the number of Jews in Law and Science, the number of blacks in basketball and entertainment, the number of Asians who earned black-belt karate kas, the number of women in nursing and child care. For meeting these kinds of goals, aggressive affirmative action programs are needed, involving reverse discrimination. The state would have to engage in intensive social engineering, intruding on personal liberty.

But, of course, the Equal Opportunity = Equal Results thesis is highly controversial, denying the legitimacy of cultural differences, family autonomy, and differences in hereditary and environmental influences. But there are strong arguments for allowing each of these factors to exist, which brings the equal opportunity = equal results thesis into question. The doctrine of equal results for groups denies the individualistic component that is at the very heart of the ideal of equal opportunity, summed up in the principle of humanity. We should be judged as individuals according to our character and talents, not according to our race, ethnicity, or gender. If the idea of equal results is not a moral goal, then the types of equal opportunity that we are interested in are versions of meritocratic and procedural equal opportunity. To get a better understanding of the value of these forms of equal opportunity, we turn to argument for and, then, against the thesis.

Arguments for Equal Opportunity

Traditionally, four arguments have been given in support of the justification of equal opportunity.

1. Equal opportunity can be justified as producing efficiency. We want the best skilled people in positions consistent with the effective execution of social

processes. We want the best political statesmen to represent us in government, the best officers to lead our armies, the most qualified airline pilots to fly our planes, the best surgeons to operate on our loved ones and ourselves, the best athletes to play on our team, the best judges in our courts, and the best teachers in our schools. All things being equal, a business that employs merely minimally capable workers will lose out to one that employs workers with high talent. We may speak of this as micro-efficiency, the meritocratic approach that rewards the best qualified person for the job in question.

But overall group merit or macro-efficiency may sometimes be antagonistic to equal opportunity for the individual (micro-efficiency). Consider this example: you and I are competing for the position of shortstop on a baseball team. You are clearly the better shortstop, though I am pretty good and am more than minimally qualified to play the position. But we also need a left fielder and you are the best person for that position—far better than I who has difficulty judging long high fly balls. The team may decide that our group efficiency will be maximized if I am assigned the shortstop position and you left field, in spite of the equal opportunity rule that would judge on individual merit. So sometimes aggregate efficiency, a function of utility, overrides the ideal of equal opportunity, but on the whole the principle of efficiency will support a presumption in favor of assigning positions to those most talented in the micro-efficiency sense.

2. Equal opportunity is justified by a notion of desert. There exists a deeply felt principle that people deserve to be treated in ways that follow from relevant antecedent activities. Equals should be treated equally according to their merits. Whereas the efficiency argument is teleological, forward looking, the desert argument is deontological, backward looking. In virtually every known culture, people think that criminals should be punished in proportion to the seriousness of their crimes and that equal work deserves equal pay. Desert implies a notion of fittingness between effort and results. It seems intuitively obvious to most people that the good should prosper and that the evil should suffer—that the punishment should fit the crime. This is expressed in the major religions. The New Testament reads (Gal. 6:7): "Whatsoever a man sows that shall he also reap," and in Hinduism and Buddhism the principle of Karma assures us that our actions in this life will determine our place in the next life. "What goes around, comes around." Kant held that people should be happy in proportion to their moral goodness.

Desert, though generally consistent with efficiency, will occasionally be antagonistic to it—as in the case of the two baseball players who compete for shortstop (discussed above). Sometimes, it seems morally right to override desert claims for other considerations. If the baseball example doesn't convince you, then how about a military one. You and I are competing to be the general who leads a division across a desert landscape against the enemy. You are clearly the best person for the job, but I am also very good (suppose you are Patton and I am Montgomery). But we also have need of a general to lead a division of troops over mountainous terrain. I happen to get altitude sickness, so only you can do this effectively. Considerations of utility would tend to override individual desert claims here and assign you to the mountains and me to the desert. Suppose the mountainous mission is far more dangerous. It's unlucky for you that you don't get altitude sickness.

3. Equal opportunity enables people to develop their talents to the utmost. William Galston puts it this way:

> When a society devotes resources to education and training, when it encourages individuals to believe that their life chances will be significantly related to their accomplishments, and when it provides an attractive array of choices, that is good reason to believe that individuals will be moved to develop some portion of their innate capacities. Thus, it may be argued, equality of opportunity is the principle of task allocation most conducive to the crucial element of the human good.[10]

As Galston points out, however, this is a very general justification and is not an absolute. Sometimes, personal development requires that we risk allowing the less qualified person to have the opportunity to develop his or her skills. We might rotate leadership for the general social good rather than allow only the single best leader to govern. We put term limits on the U.S. presidency, not necessarily because we judge an incumbent unworthy in his own right, but because of considerations such as the dangers inherent in the entrenchment of power. You may be a superior artist to me, but if artistic development is vital to my fulfilling my potential as a person, I should be given the resources to do so. The policy of universal basic education is based on the thesis that in modern society, numeracy, literacy, and basic critical skills are required for even a minimally adequate life.

4. Equal opportunity promotes personal satisfaction. By allowing people to compete for prizes and places, society promotes individual fulfillment. In this way, equal opportunity promotes excellence—if you strive for the highest achievement, you will experience deep satisfaction in attaining it. Of course, there are dangers here, for people may aim at things they have no chance at attaining and be doomed to disappointment. There is no social good without the risk of evil. Excellence, self-discipline, and commitment, which equal opportunity supports, are all good things, but they do not guarantee against foolish calculations, failure, and envy in others who, by comparing themselves unfavorably with their betters, come to loathe them. But envy is a vice that can be offset by moral education and the ideal of desert. Even if you are a better student or basketball player than I, I can be a worthy member of our society by living an exemplary moral life, fully deserving all the benefits of our society. But, of course, the risks of equal opportunity point to some objections, which we must now examine.

Objections to Equal Opportunity

Several philosophers have attacked the idea of equal opportunity either as violating the right of free association (Nozick), as misleadingly egalitarian (Schaar), or as inherently contradictory (Fishkin). Let us briefly examine each charge.

Nozick's Life Is Not a Race Objection. Nozick attacks equal opportunity because it violates the libertarian ideal of freedom to choose, our right to freedom of association. Life is not a race with a starting line, a finish line, a designated umpire, and a set of talents to be measured. Rather, individuals choose activities and exchange goods and should be left alone as long as they are not engaged in force or fraud. As an employer, I have the right to hire whomever I wish to—whether or not he or she is the most competent—even as society recognizes that I am free to marry whomever I please (with her consent). Nozick asks us to consider this example. 26 men and 26 women each want to get married.

> For each sex, all of that sex agree on the same ranking of the 26 members of the opposite sex in terms of desirability as marriage partners: call them A to Z and A' to Z' respectively in decreasing preferential order. A and A' voluntarily choose to get married, each preferring the other to any other partner. B would most prefer to marry A'. And B' would prefer to marry A, but by their choices A and A' have removed these options. When B and B' marry, their choices are not made nonvoluntarily merely by the fact that there is something else they each would rather do. The other most preferred option requires the cooperation of others who have chosen, as their right, not to cooperate. B and B' chose among fewer options than did A and A'. This contraction of the range of options continues down the line until we come to Z and Z', who each face a choice between marrying each other and remaining unmarried. Each prefers anyone of the 25 other partners who by their choices have removed themselves from consideration by Z and Z'. Z and Z' voluntarily choose to marry each other. The fact that their only other alternative is (in their view) much worse, and the fact that others chose to exercise their rights in certain ways, thereby having the external environment of oppositions in which Z and Z' choose, does not mean they did not marry voluntarily. (*Anarchy, State and Utopia*, p. 263)

Accordingly, we can have freedom to choose without having equal opportunity with other people.

Equal opportunity—like other liberal interventions—prohibits capitalist acts between consenting adults. If I want to hire my son or daughter or best friend instead of a more qualified stranger, that's my business, not the state's. We have a right to free association, which is absolute.

The right to freedom of association is important, and perhaps the state does violate it in forcing some businesses to hire applicants against the wishes of entrepreneurs. It seems that as activities become more purely personal, like the choice of marriage partners or friends, personal liberty, involving the freedom of association, increases, but as the activity becomes more public, the nondiscriminatory principle of equal opportunity increases. Where agencies are functions of the state or where they receive sizable support from the government, the principle of freedom of association ought to give way to more impartial criteria; employment should be on the basis of merit alone, according to the doctrine of equal opportunity.

Galston offers the following criticism of Nozick's libertarian proposal:

> Within every community, certain kinds of abilities are generally prized. Being excluded from an equal chance to develop them means that one is unlikely to have much of value to exchange with others: consider the problem of hard-core unemployment when the demand for unskilled labor is declining. To be sure, there is more than one social context, but the number is limited. In a society in which rising educational credentials are demanded even for routine tasks, exclusion from the competition for education and training—or inclusion on terms that amount to a handicap—will make it very difficult to enter the system of exchange. Equality of opportunity acknowledges these prerequisites to full participation in social competition, and it therefore legitimates at least some of the social interventions needed to permit full participation.[11]

Schaar's Communitarian Objection. From a socialist or communitarian perspective, Schaar offers a different criticism of the doctrine of equal opportunity. According to Schaar, equal opportunity actually supports a trend to decadence and social destruction:

> The facile formula of equal opportunity quickens that trend. It opens more and more opportunities for more and more people to contribute more and more energies toward the realization of a mass, bureaucratic, technological, privatized, materialistic, bored, and thrill-seeking, consumption-oriented society—a society of well-fed, congenial, and sybaritic monkeys surrounded by gadgets and pleasure-toys.[12]

Furthermore, the policy of equal opportunity has the ironic tendency of increasing inequalities among people:

> In previous ages, when opportunities were restricted to those of the right birth and station, it is highly probable, given the fact that nature seems to delight in distributing many traits in the pattern of a normal distribution, and given the phenomenon of regression toward the mean, that many of those who enjoyed abundant opportunities to develop their talents actually lacked the native ability to benefit from their advantages. It is reasonable to suppose that many members of ascribed elites, while appearing far superior to the ruck, really were not that superior in actual attainment. Under the regime of equal opportunity, however, only those who genuinely are superior in the desired attributes will enjoy rich opportunities to develop their qualities. This would produce, within a few generations, a social system where the members of the elites really were immensely superior in ability and attainment to the masses. We should then have a condition where the natural and social aristocracies would be identical—a meritocracy (231–2).

So equality of opportunity actually increases the gap between the elites and the ordinary folk. This is bad for democracy, for it will inevitably result in the elite ruling, dominating the lives of the poor.

But here I find a problem in Schaar's analysis. He rails against the equal opportunity, both because it serves the decadent ends of our decadent social order and because it produces a meritocratic elite. These seem quite different and opposing items. If it is the decadence of the culture he deplores, won't equal opportunity for meritocracy provide a possibility of leadership that can change the direction of society for the better? Isn't one of the problems of our democracy precisely that we often have mediocre leaders? that we lack a natural aristocracy, Plato's philosopher-king, to lead us? What is bad is the decadence, not the equal opportunity. Equal opportunity for excellence may be the only way to save us from the dangers and destruction that perennially face us. What is important is that we produce leaders who are not "sybaritic" [i.e., voluptuary, luxury loving] monkeys but moral and intellectual giants—and if equal opportunity does separate the excellent from the mediocre and ruck, why is that necessarily bad? As long as the latter are living morally and contentedly, no harm is done if they are not put in positions of power. They may still have equal protection of the law, a vote, and their basic needs met.

But Schaar thinks that our problem is deeper. He has no trouble with temporary functional inequalities, such as the authority of a teacher over his or her students, the duty of the teacher being to transmit his subject matter to the students and to become unnecessary. Competition as we have it in our society only guarantees the equal right to inequality:

> The doctrine of equal opportunity, followed seriously, removes the question of how men should be treated from the realm of human responsibility and returns it to "nature." What is so generous about telling a man he can go as far as his talents will take him when his talents are meager? Imagine a footrace of one mile in which ten men compete, with the rules being the same for all. Three of the competitors are forty years old, five are overweight, one has weak ankles, and the tenth is Roger Bannister—the first man to run the four-minute mile. What sense does it make to say that all ten have an equal opportunity to win the race? The outcome is predetermined by nature, and nine of the competitors will call it a mockery when they are told that all have the same opportunity to win (p. 233).

What are we to make of this? One can question the basic metaphor—life is not a single race. There are many races, and if we have a low probability of winning in one, there are always others. If I am not good at football, I can take up physics, if not physics, nursing; if not nursing, carpentry; if not carpentry, garbage collector. But suppose I am not first at any of these. Isn't it still reassuring to know that I am contributing to the commonweal, that I am a morally responsible person, doing my best and not being a drag on society? Why is it not permissible to lose in some race—say that I am person Z on Nozick's list of eligible bachelors, who must be content with marrying Z'? Z' and I, together with our progeny, may produce the best family in the community.

Schaar seems to think that winners must automatically dominate or exploit losers. Even if there is a tendency for power to corrupt, it can be offset by checks and balances, by protection of human rights, and by training the superior to be virtuous and kind.

A variation of Schaar's criticism argues that formal equal opportunity is not sufficient to ensure justice. Bernard Williams asks us to imagine a society that has been dominated for generations by a warrior class. At some point the proponents of equal opportunity win reforms; people will henceforth be chosen on the basis of competition which tests warrior skills. A procedurally fair competition is set in place, but the children of the warrior class, having had the advantage of superior training conditions, still win.[13]

The defenders of equal opportunity will respond to Williams that there is a difference between formal equal opportunity and the substantive type which levels the playing field so that talent alone will be rewarded. Accordingly, we must aim at the latter, which may involve providing extra educational or training opportunities to the less advantaged.

But leveling the playing field may not be so easy . The most interesting criticism of equal opportunity along these lines is set forth by James Fishkin, to which we now turn.[14]

Fishkin's Trilemma. Fishkin, drawing on examples like Williams' warrior class illustration, argues that there is something contradictory about the notion of equal opportunity—at least in the form in which it is held by many contemporary liberals. For liberals seem to want three things in their policies: equal life chances for all citizens; positions assigned by merit in fair competition; and family autonomy. Here is Fishkin's description of these ideals.

Equality of life chances: The prospects of children for eventual positions in the society should not vary in any systematic and significant manner with their arbitrary native characteristics.

Merit: There should be widespread procedural fairness in the evaluation of qualifications for positions.

The autonomy of the family: Consensual relations within a given family governing the development of its children should not be coercively interfered with except to ensure for the children the essential prerequisites for adult participation in the society.

Fishkin then argues that given the reality of unequal abilities in individuals and unequal conditions in families, a trilemma obtains. We can satisfy two but not all three of these principles. Suppose we aim at providing children with equal life chances and also decide to distribute positions by merit. Since children receive unequal benefits in families, we will have to abolish the family in order to realize this sort of equal opportunity. We would have to devise a system of collectivized child rearing similar to that described in Plato's *Republic* in order to offset the differential investments of families in their children.

This option will no doubt seem morally unacceptable to most of us. We look upon the family as one of those institutions necessary for human flourishing. We should be allowed to invest our resources in our children, and the state should not penalize us for doing so. Suppose you decide to limit your family to two children and invest all your resources in their education, and suppose your neighbors choose to have ten children and provide only minimal resources for them, spending their money on boats or gambling. If our theory of psychological development is correct—that the early years make an enormous difference in child development—there is no way that the state can make up the difference in life chances between the two sets of children. Short of abolishing the family or the practice of rewarding positions by merit, unequal life chances will result.

If the family as an institution is to be retained, we are faced with a choice: give up either the ideal of equal life chances or the ideal of meritocracy. If we continue to hold to the ideal of equal life chances together with family autonomy, we will have to sacrifice merit-based policies and adopt policies of affirmative action for those coming from less privileged homes. But this has serious drawbacks. For one thing, if carried out consistently, it will no doubt result in mediocrity and inefficiency. Related to mediocrity, families lose incentive to provide a good education for their children, for parents will reason that the best way to help their children in the long run is to deprive them, so that the state will compensate the children for their disadvantage.

Finally, if we value merit and excellence for utilitarian and deontological reasons, and we continue to value the family, there is no option but to give up the notion of equal life chances. But this seems a tragic choice, for the disadvantaged children are being penalized for their bad luck of being born into families with fewer resources or less ability to care.

Naturally, tradeoffs are possible: we can encourage family autonomy but supplement it with universal education, including remedial education when needed, and adopt educational enhancement programs for disadvantaged children which do not penalize families that invest their resources in their children. If we are to implement affirmative action, the rule should be: the earlier the enhancement input the better—better a head start program than race norming at the time of college admission. However, strong affirmative action directed at equal results violates the essence of equal opportunity, which focuses on the individual, not group membership. Justice, wearing her perennial blindfold weighs only one's abilities, performance, and character, not one's race or gender.[15]

Drawing on Fishkin's analysis, we can conclude that there is no way to satisfy all our legitimate social concerns in devising programs for this type of equal opportunity. Society must make difficult decisions between the ideals of equal chances, merit, and family autonomy. But one more distinction must be made, which may ameliorate the matter. With regard to positions and goods, we must separate internal goods connected with these objects from external goods, especially material rewards. Galston expresses this point well:

> A fair competition may demonstrate my qualification for a particular occupation. But the talents that so qualify me do not entitle me to whatever external

rewards happen to be attached to that occupation. I may nevertheless be entitled to them, but an independent line of argument is needed to establish that fact. So, for example, in accordance with public criteria, my technical competence may entitle me to a position as a brain surgeon. It does not follow that I am entitled to half a million dollars a year. Even if we grant what is patently counterfactual in the case of doctors—that compensation is determined by the market—the principle of task assignment in accordance with talents does not commit us to respect market outcomes. Indeed, the kind of competition inherent in a system of equal opportunity bears no clear relation to the competition characteristic of the market.

The distinction has an important consequence. Many thinkers oppose meritocratic systems on the ground that there is no reason why differences of talent should generate or legitimate vast differences in material rewards. They are quite right. But this is not an objection to meritocracy as such. It is an objection to the way society assigns rewards to tasks, not to the way it assigns individuals to tasks.[16]

This seems, at least partly, correct. Meritocracy aims at placing excellent people in social positions, and this does not in itself entail commensurate material rewards. Unfortunately, it is hard to separate excellence from material rewards. As John Searle has said "Money attracts talent." One of the main incentives for developing excellence is the promise of material advantage. Market forces encourage meritocracy, but merit often seeks tangible rewards. Equal life chances, as Fishkin has pointed out, become impossible if we hold to the values of merit and family autonomy. We cannot have our cake and eat it too. The best we can obtain is a workable compromise of competing ideals.

Conclusion

Our arguments for equal opportunity seem cogent in that they take the individual seriously as the basic unit of moral and political consideration. Equal opportunity focuses on the individual's abilities and development, not on his or her race, ethnicity, or family pedigree. The problem is that there are several different conceptions of equal opportunity: arbitrary, meritocratic, procedural, and result-oriented. Arbitrary opportunity seems a violation of our rational nature, and substantive result-oriented opportunity seems a violation of the very notion of opportunity as focusing on the individual as the basic unit of moral consideration. Fishkin's analysis, the weightiest of the objections discussed, helps us see that pure equal opportunity is impossible. The most coherent versions of equal opportunity seem to lie in the area of meritocratic and procedural policies. Taking equal opportunity seriously entails reform of our basic institutions in order to make them more respondent to human needs and potential, but it still distributes offices according to talent and merit. Equal opportunity, though it is not the only value related to justice, is a necessary condition for justice.

Notes

1. Peter Westen, "The Concept of Equal Opportunity" in *Ethics* 95 9 (July 1985), 837–50, reprinted in L. P. Pojman and R. Westmoreland, eds., *Equality: Selected Readings* (Oxford University Press, 1997).

2. John Schaar, "Equal Opportunity and Beyond" in *Nomos IX: Equality* (Atherton Press, 1967), 228–49. Reprinted in Pojman and Westmoreland, *Equality*.

3. William Galston, "A Liberal Defense of Equal Opportunity" in *Justice and Equality: Here and Now*, ed. Frank S. Lucash (Cornell University Press, 1986). Reprinted in Pojman and Westmoreland, *Equality*. The discussion in the following section is indebted to Galston's article.

4. Jorges Luis Borges, "The Lottery in Babylon" in *Labyrinths* (New York: New Direction Books, 1964).

5. Douglas Rae et al.. *Equalities* (Cambridge, MA: Harvard University Press, 1981), p. 61.

6. Hochschild, p 94.

7. In *Equal Set of Skills*, Hochschild writes: "Such internal means, which change the character or personality of their recipient, could range from teaching all first-graders that reading is fun to ensuring that all adults are equally talented and ambitious. The institutional mechanisms could run from Boy Scout troops to Kurt Vonnegut's Handicapper-General. Most debates over this more extensive form of equal opportunity focus on deciding how much energy and resources the state should devote to equalizing a few critically important skills." Hochschild, *op. cit.*, p. 98.

8. Hochschild, p. 99.

9. John Rawls, *A Theory of Justice* (Cambridge, MA: Harvard University Press, 1971), pp. 83–4.

10. Galston, "A Liberal Defense."

11. Ibid.

12. Schaar, "Equal Opportunity and Beyond."

13. Bernard Williams, "The Idea of Equality" in Peter Laslett and W. G. Runciman, eds., *Philosophy, Politics and Society*. Series II (London: Basil Blackwell, 1962), 110–31. Reprinted in Pojman and Westmoreland, *Equality*.

14. James Fishkin, "Liberty Versus Equal Opportunity" in *Social Philosophy & Policy* 5:1 (1978) : 32–48. Reprinted in Pojman and Westmoreland, *Equality*.

15. Many people do not realize that the civil rights movement was essentially a meritocratic equal opportunity movement and that the 1964 Civil Rights Act promised not to require preferential treatment for any group. "No employer is required to grant preferential treatment to any individual or group on account of any imbalance which may exist between the total number or percentage of persons of such race, color, religion, sex, or national origin in any community, state, section, or other area" (Title VII of the *Civil Rights Act of 1964*).

16. Galston, "A Liberal Defense."

CHAPTER 7

Global Justice

> Whatever a man has in superabundance is owed, of natural right, to the poor for their sustenance.
>
> (Thomas Aquinas)

> When anyone asked [Diogenes] which country he came from, he said, 'I am a citizen of the world'
>
> (Diogenes Laertius, on Diogenes the Cynic)

Introduction: Global Disparities

According to the *United Nations Development Report*, one-fifth of the world, about 1.2 billion people, lives in dire poverty. Half the world lives on less than $1 per day. While 61 percent of Americans, almost 200 million people, are overweight, 170 million people in the Third World are seriously underweight. Most of these are children who, if they fail to receive adequate nourishment, will either die or suffer brain damage.[1] Americans raised over $1.3 billion for relief of the families of victims of the terrorist attacks on September 11, 2001. A total of $353 million was raised for the families of the 400 police officers and firefighters who died trying to save others. That comes to $880,000 for each family, families that would have been provided for by New York City and state pension and insurance plans. Furthermore, the Red Cross decided to provide financial aid (the equivalent of three months rent) plus money for utilities and groceries, for anyone living in the lower Manhattan area who claimed to have been affected by the destruction of the World Trade Center. It set up card tables in the lobbies of expensive apartment buildings in Tribeca, where wealthy financiers, stockbrokers, lawyers, and rock stars live, to offer the residents these financial donations. The higher their income, the larger the financial award. Some got as much as $10,000. Meanwhile, 30,000 children in other parts of the world die every day of hunger and preventable diseases. Oxfam International was not overwhelmed with financial support for their work.[2]

Whereas life expectancy in the developed countries is around seventy-seven years, in the undeveloped countries it is around forty-seven years, and in some cases even lower. One in five children dies before reaching the age of five in the developing nations, compared to one in one hundred in the developed world. While many people in the developed nations live in luxury, poverty, disease, hunger, and premature death are rampant in the Third World. In the United States with a projected federal budget for 2003 of over $2.1 trillion, $34 billion are spent on alcoholic beverages and $50 billion on entertainment, while we give only $13 billion in foreign aid, less than 10 cents on every $100.[3]

What does justice require regarding distant and future people, especially people who are suffering from hunger or disease in other lands, strangers to us, except for reports by world health organizations or the evening news? Do we have positive obligations to them? In this chapter we will consider both arguments *for* and *against* the proposition that we have considerable obligations to other people and nations.

Theories of Obligation to Distant People

Nationalists and contractarians (those who hold our only obligations are contractual ones) do not believe we have obligations to help the poor of less-developed nations. Any duties to aid the worst off must be confined to one's own fellow citizens. Other people believe such obligations should be personal and not state sponsored. Still others believe that we have a duty to help the poor of other less-developed nations, but it is not a duty of justice but of beneficence, or an act of supererogation. Finally, there are those who believe that justice requires that we help those who are suffering in other countries. But among these last named, some derive their obligation to help from *rights*, while others hold that *duties* of justice are not based on specific rights, but human rights are derivative from duties. Who is right?

Let us examine each of these positions:

The No-Obligation Thesis

We do not have obligations to help the poor of less-developed nations. It might be nice to help them, but the poor have no claims against us, nor do we have any duties to them. Two very different major political theories embrace this position: (1) libertarianism and (2) welfare liberalism.[4] Libertarians argue that all natural rights are negative, the main right being the negative right of liberty. People ought not to be coerced to do anything. As long as you are not unjustly harming other people, you should be free to do whatever you like. We have already examined libertarianism in Chapter 3 and, while it had some good features, we found it to be an inadequate position. Although liberty is a significant moral value, it is not the only moral value. Morality focuses on our social interdependence. We are all in each other's debt, so that we have, at least, minimal duties to aid those in need.

Welfare liberalism of the type set forth by John Rawls in his monumental *A Theory of Justice* (which we examined in Chapter 4) holds that the state's duty to help the worst off people (the *difference principle*) is confined to the citizens of the state and not to strangers or foreigners.[5] Rawls argues that our responsibilities to aid the worst-off people must originate in a contract that ensures mutual advantage. But we have no contractual relations with people in other countries, so we have no obligations to come to their aid. Charles Beitz has argued that Rawls's theory is simply incomplete here, for behind the *veil of ignorance*, we would not know into which nation we would be born, and so we would choose principles that w*ould* apply universally. Hence, the *difference principle* would apply to all human beings everywhere.[6] Justice would require that any inequality be justified by helping the worst off members of the global society. If one accepts the Rawlsian framework, this seems correct.

Under the classic theory of justice as desert, needs are relevant to just distribution only to the extent that they express undeserved burdens, not in their own right. To the extent that unmet, important needs are a burden to one's life and constitute a significant barrier to achieving one's life goal, they may be viewed as unjust burdens that require compensatory action. But simply having a need does not in itself demand compensation. The need for love, self-respect, health, and shelter are important, but the fact that they are unmet does not provide grounds for social compensation. A man with a chronically sick wife or child deserves compensation since, through no fault of his own, he has a greater need than others; the same is true of one who has a large family. But satisfying these needs seems more to do with benevolence than with justice.

On the other hand, unfulfilled needs for basic food and shelter, basic education, or medical service give rise to legitimate claims for their provision because they are typically within the power of society to satisfy those needs. As long as they remain unsatisfied, a person suffers major obstacles in his life, including obstacles to his individual actions in satisfying all other needs. Welfare liberals like Rawls, Charles Beitz, Henry Shue, and James Sterba are really revisionists, urging us to extend the notion of justice to include essential subsistence needs.

Justice creates a new basic right to subsistence. We have a right to those things that we require if we are to survive and to have any sort of a life worth living. The criteria of what is a basic need vary as a function of geography and the culture of a society.

But classic theorists will argue that we may not need such an extension of justice, creating new subsistence rights. We might argue that a moral-political philosophy grounded in our common humanity would deny that rights are necessary for generating moral obligations to aid other people.

The No-State Obligation Thesis

The state has no duty to render foreign aid. Many people agree that we have duties to help the poor in other countries, but deny that the state should be involved. If individuals gave sufficiently to famine relief and helping the poor, perhaps the state would not be required to get involved in foreign aid, but a modern state like the United States has enormous resources at its disposal so that, if it can do so efficiently, it ought to render assistance to needy people in other nations. States are artificial persons, institutions that may be held accountable for their actions. They can carry out unjust acts of aggression, as the German government did in World War II, or they can come to the aid of suffering people as the United States did with its Marshall Plan after that war, assisting in the economic rebuilding of Europe. The fact is that we give very little to help people in developing nations— about 0.1% of our total economic product, a much smaller percentage than the

Scandinavian countries. But private charity produces even less. While the U.S. budget allocates $10 billion for foreign aid, about 10 cents to every $100 of our GNP (which amounts to over $2 trillion), private charity provides about $4 billion or 4 cents for every $100. At the very least we ought to aid developing countries in establishing democratic governments and then helping democratic regimes to help themselves in improving the conditions of their people. The affluent countries of the world are incredibly rich. They have enormous surpluses, some of which should be used to alleviate misery in poor countries. If states are artificial persons, then if individuals have obligations to give some of their surplus wealth to ameliorate the suffering of less fortunate human beings in other lands, so do states.

The Beneficence Thesis

This theory, held by utilitarians but also by other philosophers, holds that it is good to aid those in need, but it is not a requirement of justice. It is a duty of beneficence or even merely a supererogatory act. Beneficence has to do with charity, generosity, with good will. Justice, as we have seen, is a more stringent requirement, having to do with redistributing burdens and benefits, according to some criterion such as desert, need, right, or contribution. Justice creates a specific right on the part of the beneficiary in a way that beneficence often does not, though beneficence can be even more demanding on the agent, as the discussion will now illustrate. If we believe that a common humanity holds us together in a common bond, so that we have *prima facie* obligations to help each other, then it follows that we ought to endeavor to provide every human being with a minimal level of subsistence.

To see what is involved in helping distant people, consider two scenarios based on thought experiments given by Peter Unger.[7]

The Envelope. Suppose you receive an envelope from a highly respectable charity, such as UNICEF, with a letter explaining that thousands of children are dying of dehydration and diarrhetic diseases. It explains that unless you send in a check for $100, then over thirty more children will die soon of dehydration. But you throw the material into your trash can, so that thirty children die, who would have been saved.

Have you done anything seriously wrong? Most students Unger has asked say no. My students concur. You haven't done anything wrong by simply throwing away the letter, requesting a donation. But now turn to the case of Bob's *Bugatti* (a rare automobile often worth $1 million).

Bob's Bugatti. Bob is close to retirement. He's worked hard all his life and has hardly enough money to live on for retirement, except for owning an expensive Bugatti, one of the few mint-conditioned Bugattis in the world (valued at $1 million), which is likely to appreciate at 20% per year, securing him a comfortable retirement. If the Bugatti is somehow stolen or destroyed, Bob will have a hard time making ends meet for the rest of his life, though if he is frugal, he probably will live a minimally decent life, eating simply but without luxuries.

On a rural road near the garage where it's securely kept, Bob's gone for a careful drive in his Bugatti. At a certain point he spies a tiny shiny object. To inspect it, Bob parks the car in the only place from where he can proceed on foot for a close encounter, a parking place that's just 10 yards beyond the end of a trolley track. When Bob walks over to the shiny object, he finds it's a switch that can be set in two ways. And, as Bob observes, there's a trolley up the line that's barreling toward the switch's fork. As the shiny switch is set, the trolley will go down the fork's opposite side, not the branch leading to a spot near Bob's Bugatti. But, as Bob notices, on that side there's a young child trapped on the track. Bob realizes that he has two options: If he does nothing about the situation, the child will be killed, but he'll enjoy a comfortable retirement. If he changes the switch's settings (his second option), then, while nobody's killed, after rolling down the vacant branch and beyond the track's end, the trolley will totally destroy Bob's uninsurable Bugatti, wiping out his entire retirement fund. What should Bob do?

Almost everyone agrees that Bob should save the child and accept the loss of his $1 million mint vehicle. It would be a cruel disregard of life to put one's car ahead of a child. But is this answer consistent with the answer to the *Envelope* case? In that case, by failing to send in a $100 check to the charity, you fail to do what will save the lives of thirty children. In Bob's case only one child will die for deciding to save a $1 million car.

It would seem that we who have more money than we need to live a moderately decent life in an affluent Western society have an obligation to share our super-abundance with those who are in dire need. Unger does not appeal to justice to generate a duty to aid those in dire need. His argument seems to be based on working out the implications of our basic moral values. They seem especially conducive to utilitarianism. But his view was long ago set forth by John Locke as a principle of charity. In his *First Treatise on Government* (1688), Locke wrote:

> But we know God has not let man so to the mercy of another, that he may starve him if he please: God the Lord and Father of all, has given no one of his children such a property, in his portion of the things of the world, but that he has given his needy brother a right to the surplusage of his goods; so that it cannot be denied him, when his pressing wants call for it. And therefore no man could ever have a just power over the life of another, by right of property in land or possessions; since it could always be a sin in any man of estate, to let his brother perish for want of affording him relief out of his plenty. As *Justice* gives every man a title to the product of his honest industry and the fair acquisition of his ancestors descended to him; so *Charity* gives every man a title to so much out of another's plenty, as will keep him from extreme want, where he has no means to subsist otherwise. (Locke's *First Treatise on Government*, 1688; #42)

We have a duty, based on charity, to alleviate the suffering of people wherever they are suffering. The moral life requires that we live simply so that others may simply live. We should give intelligently, supporting programs with lower overhead and minimal bureaucracy that are more efficient in ameliorating suffering, giving to programs that will enable the needy to become self-sufficient, including the means of controlling their population growth. We should give to international aid groups and give more than most of us do.

The Justice Thesis

Finally, we come to the view that justice, not merely charity, requires that we help those who are suffering in other countries. Among those who hold this position, some derive their obligation to help from rights, while others hold that duties of justice are not based on specific rights, but on human rights that are derived from duties.

Justice: Theories of Rights and Duties

Those who hold that justice is rights-based argue that a set of universal human rights exists, so that everyone in need may legitimately claim that those with surplus ought to meet their needs. Those who make duties primary, on the other hand, argue that although we all have duties to help those in need, no specific needy persons have rights against us. The argument for a rights-based theory is centered mainly in *intuitionism* or in *interest theory*.[8] (1) *Intuitionism*. It strikes some people as obvious that we all have a right to equal consideration of interests, including having our basic needs met. Intuitionism has the problem of resting on no other grounds than itself, so that if you and I, as intuitionists, differ on a moral issue, say abortion or the morality of the death penalty, we have no option but to agree to disagree. Sometimes, alas, we may be unable to do more than that, but we should strive to defend our judgments with reasons, with arguments based on widely shared assumptions. (2) *Interest Theory*. Those who ground rights in interests face a problem of explaining which interests generate rights and which do not. Surely, interests create reasons for action, but a reason for action is not the same thing as a right that allows one to claim something of another person or society. So let me briefly defend the thesis that duties are foundational for rights and not vice versa.

Once more, consider the *Parable of the Good Samaritan*.[9] A man, presumably a Jew, went down from Jerusalem to Jericho and was attacked by thieves, beaten and robbed and left dying on the side of the road. Two fellow Jews, a priest and a Levite, each on his way to an appointment, pass the sufferer by "on the other side," but a Samaritan, not even a member of his ethnic-cultural community, "has compassion," approaches the man, and binds up his wounds, "pouring on oil and wine." The Samaritan takes him to an inn, where he may be healed, even paying for his expenses. Did the victim have a *right* to be cared for by the priest, Levite, and Samaritan? No mention of rights (or of *justice*, for that matter) is made. In fact, the concept of rights was not known in the classical world before the Enlightenment. Jesus describes the care given by the Samaritan as a duty of love, under the rubric of the commandment "Love thy neighbor as thyself." Who is my neighbor? The answer seems to be: Everyone in need through no fault of his own is my neighbor, regardless of his race, class, or nationality. In the parable, not his fellow countrymen, but only the stranger, fulfilled the duty to love one's neighbor. Although no mention of justice is made, the act may be described as such. The victim was an innocent man in need, and the Samaritan had the resources to aid him. If *need* is an appropriate criterion for justice, as Rawls argues, then we can say that the priest and Levite failed to do justice, but that the Samaritan acted according to justice, not simply benevolently, though he may have gone beyond the requirements of justice in paying for all the victim's treatment. The argument for rights as interests goes like this:

1. If A has an interest in having x, A has a right to x over against anyone B who can satisfy that interest. That is, B has a duty to satisfy B's interest.
2. A has an interest in having x.
3. Therefore B has a duty to satisfy B's interest.

But the argument may be too strong. Surely, having an interest is a reason for action, so that B ought to consider satisfying the interest, but that is not the same thing as having a duty to do so. Interpreted broadly, antelopes have an interest not to be devoured by tigers, but we have no obligation to intervene on their behalf.

Let us turn to duty-based arguments for global justice.

Immanuel Kant distinguished between *perfect* and *imperfect duties*. Perfect duties are absolute and universally binding, such as not taking innocent life, intentionally injuring others, or breaking a promise, whereas imperfect duties allow discretion regarding how and to what extent the individual will fulfill them. For example, I have a duty to develop my talents, but I may exercise discretion as to which talents I develop and to what degree. Most perfect duties are negative, while imperfect duties are all positive. For example, our negative duty to refrain from killing an innocent person is more stringent than our positive duty to help someone in need. Rights are correlative to perfect duties but not imperfect ones.

Accordingly, I have an imperfect duty to contribute to the amelioration of suffering, but there are innumerable ways in which I can do this, so that no particular sufferer can claim a right to my care—unless I have a special relationship with that sufferer (say I caused the suffering unjustly or am a close relation to her). Suppose the Good Samaritan had come upon 100 people in dire need but with resources available to aid only ten. He would have leeway as to which ten to help. None of the 100 have a claim on his resources. It is left to his discretion to choose the ten that are to be helped. Kant (Mill and W. D. Ross held similar positions) seems correct here. Morality is centered in our duties to carry out the moral law or promote the human good, and some of these duties entail specific rights on the part of others.

A second argument for the priority of duties over rights concerns the duty to render to people according to their deserts (see Chapter 2). One dominant requirement of justice is to give every person his or her due, but desert is not the same as a right. John may deserve to win the race, since he is the best runner and worked the hardest to win, but if Joe outperforms him by some luck (say John has a cramp or trips), Joe has the right to the prize, not the more deserving John. It seems odd to say that the criminal who deserves a certain punishment for a crime has a *right* to that punishment or that the hardest worker in the company has an entitlement to a raise. The virtuous generally deserve to be happier than the vicious, but they are not entitled to that comparative happiness, nor can they demand that society provide them with happiness or even the comparative resources to make it so.

A third argument for the priority of duties over rights is found in examining the *posterity problem*—the thesis that we have duties to future generations.[10] Rights theory requires that we have identifiable individuals as the bearers of rights, but most of us sense that we have obligations to future generations, to people not yet born. At least we have a duty not to deplete the environment to the extent that it will not be fit for prosperous human habitation in the future. But if the rights-priority thesis is correct, our intuition is misguided. We have no such duty, and the environmental movement, oriented as it is to duty to future generations, is misguided. If we have obligations to leave the world (the environment) in as good as shape as we found it, then duties are prior to rights, for the particular future bearers of right do not yet exist.

One might question this argument. Why think future people do not have rights against us? Here is a counterexample: Imagine I plant a landmine in a kindergarten classroom when I know that ten years from now a child not currently in existence will step on it and lose a leg. One may claim that my planting that landmine violated the child's right. There is a problem in determining when the violation occurred, but this is not a problem unique to the rights context.[11] So it seems that I have violated the right of a future person. What can we say in response? Surely, I have done wrong, but the question is whether the best way of describing the situation is in terms of rights-violation. Suppose that the kindergarten is torn down and no one is ever harmed when the landmine explodes. No one's rights have been violated. A duty-based system would state that we have duties not to cause unnecessary harm, so that knowingly planting the landmine is wrong because we have reason to believe that children will occupy the kindergarten at a future time. There is a high probability that people will be harmed, so I should act responsibly and refrain from leaving landmines around.

A final argument in favor of the priority of duties is that question of our relationship to animals. If rational self-consciousness is a requirement for having a right, then many animals do not have rights. But we may well have a duty not to unnecessarily harm them or cause them death or suffering. This duty flows from a general duty not to cause unnecessary suffering rather than from a focus on the rights of animals.

Rights, as Joel Feinberg has argued, are important, since they permit us to make claims, to defend our dignity before the world. Even a utopian society without rights, *Nowheresville*, would be deficient because it would prohibit individuals from making moral claims and defending their dignity against unjust discrimination.[12] This seems correct. Rights are nice. We like them because they give us things, whereas duties are onerous because they hold us accountable for our actions and demand things of us, sometimes at considerable sacrifice. Rights proceed from a legal paradigm, not a moral paradigm. The fundamental locus of rights is the entitlement created by a legal contract. If I contract to pay you $1000 a week for building my house and you build the house, you have a right to the $1000 per week. A society emphasizing our duties to each other fosters responsible behavior, whereas one emphasizing rights tends to foster impersonal, social atomism, adversarial relations, and litigation whereby lawyers, but not necessarily the rest of us, come out ahead.

The danger of rights-language is its focus on claims and compensation, whereas sometimes negotiation and care or healing and reconciliation are what is needed. So although rights have a place in our moral repertoire, serving as correlatives to duties, they should not become the central focus of our moral and political discourse. The very proliferation of rights in our society probably is a symptom of a growing anonymity and atomization, where the adversarial relationship replaces informal discussion, personal trust, and a sense of a public self in which each of us recognizes his or her social responsibility and loyalty to the society at large. We don't want to live in Feinberg's *Nowheresville*, where rights are nonexistent, but neither do we want to live in *Litigationville*, with its rights-dominated orientation, one that our society is in danger of approximating. A duty-based moral system gets the relationship just right. It seems then that rights are simply the correlative features of duties. Duties are fundamental, and rights are derivative from duties. Where we can identify a specific duty to a specific person, we can generate a corresponding right, but rights do not exist as independent of or prior to duties. Negative rights simply reflect the basic moral obligation to leave people in peace. A universal right to life means that every human being has a duty not to kill another innocent human being. A property right signifies a general duty not to steal another person's possessions.

Universal Duties of Justice

We do not need to rely on a rights-based moral theory to create duties to assist those in need wherever they be. Consider this illustration given by Henry Shue.

> A large tract of land in a rural village of an African country has been the property of a peasant family for generations. The family is comparatively well off but not rich. They grow black beans on the land, which is the main source of nourishment and protein in the village. The family employs six workers during the harvest.
>
> One day a man from the capital offers this peasant a contract that not only guarantees him annual payments for a ten-year lease on his land but also guarantees him a salary (regardless of how the crops turned out) to be the foreman for a new kind of production on his land. The new kind of production requires him to grow coffee instead of black beans. Other families accept similar contracts and the production of coffee, to be exported to Europe and the United States, replaces black beans throughout the region.
>
> With the reduction in the supply, the price of black beans skyrockets, so that people cannot afford to buy the nutrient-rich food as they had in the past. When a famine came one season, children and the elderly became weak and many died.[13]

This illustrates how through no one's direct fault the free-market mechanisms can result in tragedy. The question is, "What should be done about it?" Should capitalism be restrained? Should the richer countries come to the aid of the poor sub-Saharan region that now finds itself in dire poverty, unable to survive without input from the outside?

As Shue points out, the malnutrition resulting from the choices made in switching from black beans to coffee was not a natural disaster but a social disaster. Specific human decisions, permitted by the presence of specific social institutions and the absence of others in the context of scarcity of land upon which to grow food, resulted in the malnutrition. The Noble Prize-winning economist Amartya Sen has supported this thesis, arguing that in these sorts of circumstances, changing market conditions have led to mass starvation. Famines are often caused not by a lack of food, but by unfavorable market conditions that may cause the poor to be financially unable to procure available food.[14]

Shue puts forth a tripartite set of moral principles to cover such cases of subsistence:
We have

1. Duties not to eliminate a person's only available means of subsistence—duties to *avoid* depriving.
2. Duties to protect people against deprivation of the only available means of subsistence by other people—duties to *protect* from deprivation.
3. Duties to provide for the subsistence of those unable to provide for their own—duties to *aid* the deprived.

In Shue's account, the state should have had regulations prohibiting such contracts as were entered into by the capitalist and the peasant. But once they have been entered into and disaster strikes, the rest of us are bound by principle 3—a duty to come to the aid of the deprived people of the region and alleviate the malnutrition problem.

Shue doesn't discuss the issue of personal responsibility in such cases, but one might ask whether the peasant and the people of the region aren't responsible for the choices they made in permitting and making contracts to switch crops from black bean to coffee. Let us concede that we have a tripartite duty to try to *avoid*, *protect*, and *aid* in defeating malnutrition in poorer countries. The duty we have is a *prima facie* duty, which can be overridden by other duties, such as a duty to one's own county or more deserving poor people. At some point, the people of the region must take responsibility for their plight and live with the consequences of their decisions. If this is correct, justice, and not merely beneficence, requires that we help the poor who are suffering. Meeting needs, such as in bringing aid to famine victims and people suffering malnutrition is an imperfect duty arising from our common humanity. It is not a perfect duty that requires us to aid the people in this region, but an imperfect one. That is, we have a duty arising from benevolence to bring aid to the needy, but because many groups need our aid, and we can only help some of them, we may use discretion as to which of the poor are most deserving of our help in the present circumstances.

In a world with surplus wealth and enormous waste, however, it seems cruel and selfish not to ameliorate the staggering suffering, brought on by extreme poverty, malnutrition, and disease. Can we go so far as to say that the poor in general have a right to some of our surplus wealth? This leads us to the ideal of cosmopolitanism.

Cosmopolitan Vision

Justice, as the proper allocation of benefits and burdens, of duties and correlative rights, seems to transcend particular communities and states. As we argued in Chapter 1, justice, as an essential dimension of morality, is universal. It is impartial, treating each person as an individual who is owed equal consideration of interests. National boundaries are accidental and contingent, at best serving utilitarian purposes or protecting cultures and communities. They are not fundamental features of the moral domain in the way individuals are.

The same is true of resources. Recall our discussion of Rawls's rejection of desert as the criterion for distribution of goods because our talents "were arbitrary from a moral point of view." We may compare a nation's resources to an individual's talents and argue that the oil or diamonds under one's feet are truly arbitrary from a moral point of view. As Charles Beitz notes, "Unlike talents resources are not naturally attached to persons. [They] do not stand in the same relation to personal identity as to talents. It would be inappropriate to take the sort of pride in the diamond deposits in one's own backyard that one takes in the ability to play *Appassionata*."[15]

Just as our basic moral duties to individuals do not depend on nationality, so meeting human need through redistributing resources does not depend on nationality either. Just as the Good Samaritan cared for a Jew, a member of a rival community and nation, so we ought to provide for the basic needs of distant people, those victims of famine, war, and disease, whatever their nationality. Similarly, if you see a child drowning, you do not ask her for her citizen papers or passport before you rescue her. You save her because she is a human being in need and you can do great good with a minimum of sacrifice. The principle of humanity, implicit in this illustration, is the very basis of the moral point of view.

Charles Darwin articulated this view over a century ago in what we may call *the expanding circle* thesis.

> As man advances in civilization, and small tribes are united into larger communities, the simplest reason would tell each individual that he ought to extend his social instincts and sympathies to all the members of the same nation, though personally unknown to him. This point being once reached, there is only an artificial barrier to prevent his sympathies extending to the men of all nations and races. If, indeed, such men are separated from him by greater differences in appearance or habits, experience unfortunately shows us how long it is, before we look at them as our fellow-creatures. Sympathy beyond the confines of man, that is, humanity to the lower animals, seems to

be one of the latest acquisitions. It is apparently unfelt by savages, except towards their pets. How little the old Romans knew of it is shown by their abhorrent gladiatorial exhibitions. The very idea of humanity, as far as I could observe, was new to most of the Gauchos of the Pampas. This virtue, one of the noblest with which man is endowed, seems to arise incidentally from our sympathies becoming more tender and more widely diffused, until they are extended to all sentient beings. As soon as the virtue is honored and practiced by some few men, it spreads through instruction and example to the young, and eventually becomes incorporated in public opinion.[16]

The metaphor of the expanding circle best describes our expanding moral relationships. We have primary obligations to our family and friends, then to our neighbors and the members of our community, then to our fellow citizens, and then to all humans everywhere. We also have duties to animals, but these may consist primarily in negative duties. Continuing with this metaphor, we can argue that we have expanding obligations to meet the needs of distant people. We can reason in the following manner.

If my family member needs some good and I have the resources to provide that good without doing anything immoral, I ought to provide my family member with the good. If my family member's basic needs are met and my neighbor's family member has a need which I can meet at no great cost to my family and if no one else is meeting that need, I ought to meet that need. If my family member's needs and my neighbor's family member's needs have been met, and a stranger has a need that I can meet at no great cost, I ought to meet the stranger's need. Of course, we may qualify the claim to have one's needs met by another. If my neighbor or the stranger (or even my family member) is in need through his own negligence or misuse of his resources (e.g., he gave in to alcohol or gambling), he does not deserve to be helped and I am released from my obligation. I may have an obligation to help the neighbor's children who are innocent victims of their parents' vicious waste, and I may be merciful and forgiving toward the neighbor's irresponsible behavior, but I don't have an obligation to sacrifice my own resources for his good. Of course, it is usually hard to be sure that neighbors and strangers have been wasteful of their resources, so the presumption is that they are innocent until proven guilty.

If we apply this rationale to distant people, those suffering in underdeveloped countries, their plight is analogous to that of the needy stranger in our own country. Justice requires that, unless there is evidence that the sufferers have been irresponsible with their resources, we must use some of our surplus resources to alleviate their most urgent needs. Of course, the best help we can give is long-term assistance in self-help. "Give a man a fish and tomorrow he'll still need another fish. Teach a man to fish and tomorrow he'll catch a fish for himself." So while we have obligations to aid the more than 1 billion people in the world who are severely malnourished, relieving their immediate needs, we ought also to help them develop self-sustaining economic processes and institutions.

Those who make rights prior to duties presume that human beings have basic needs without which they cannot live or find a worthwhile life. This is true, but, note well, that there may be no one in a position to meet these basic needs. It seems more accurate to say that rights are correlative to duties so that since *ought implies can*, where there is a need that can be met and no excusing conditions obtain, where there is a need the rest of us have an obligation to try to meet that need. When a society becomes affluent, it may legislate that all citizens be accorded a right to a minimal level of well-being, of welfare, so that the state has a duty to provide for minimal welfare.

Let me sum up our argument to this point. The moral point of view, whether one takes a consequentialist or deontological perspective, is universalistic, based on rationally approved, impartial principles, recognizing a universal humanity rather than particular groups or persons, as the bearers of moral consideration. As we noted earlier, when seeing a child drowning, we do not ask him, "Are you an American?" before seeking to save him. We rescue him or her because he or she is a human being. We must come to see all humanity as tied together in a common moral network. If all do not hang together, each will *hang* alone. Since morality is inherently universalistic, its primary focus must be on the individual, not the nation, race, or religious group. In Chapter 5 we argued that justice requires attempting to provide each person with equal opportunity to live a worthwhile life. Every person has a *prima facie* right to the conditions that would enable one to develop his potential to a reasonable degree. This statement is usually taken to mean "to provide each citizen within a nation with that opportunity." But why confine the notion to nation-states? Shouldn't the principle be extended to include every human being throughout the world and those yet to be born? We generally believe that it is unjust for someone to have fewer opportunities to develop his or her life because of morally irrelevant traits, such as race, ethnicity, cultural identity, religion, or gender. If so, shouldn't we add nationality to the list of morally irrelevant characteristics? If one goal of morality is to promote each person's flourishing, shouldn't we transcend national boundaries and seek to apply the principle of equal opportunity to all people everywhere? Perhaps the main reason for our failure to do so has to do with our lack of moral imagination. Granted, it would be a *prima facie* duty (with a correlative right), able to be overridden by other duties or prevented from being realized by recalcitrant social conditions (e.g., the indigenous culture is antidemocratic and oppressive and cannot be changed without high costs), but it would still be part of our moral repertoire and, as such, guide public policy. We are all human beings, and only accidentally, citizens of the United States, Afghanistan, Germany, Japan, Brazil, Rwanda, or Nigeria. Many of us are grateful to be Americans, but we didn't earn this property, and we should recognize that our common humanity overrides specific racial, nationalistic identity. A global perspective ought to replace nationalism and tribalism as the *leitmotif* of ethical living. A rational ethic, based in universal human values, must become the underpinning of a renewed cosmopolitanism. If this argument is sound, justice, at least in a world of affluence such as ours, creates a *prima facie* right to equal opportunity, including the right to the basic conditions for living a worthwhile life, where nutrition, minimal health care, and security are available to all.

Today the threats to morality come from fundamentalist religious particularism, naive egoism, and ethical relativism, all of which eschew universal morality and lead to moral nihilism. A defensible moral objectivism, the core of which is accepted by a consensus of moral philosophers, must permeate our society as well as every society under the sun. At present, most people derive their moral principles from their culture, their religion, or their narrow tribal ideology. An educational process inculcating universal norms in people everywhere is a crucial task for the leaders of the twenty-first century. Principles, such as forbidding murder (the unjust killing of innocents), dishonesty, and exploitation and promoting reciprocal cooperation, freedom, and universal justice must be seen as the necessary conditions for the good life, civilization, and peace. The cosmopolitan thesis about justice that I have been defending requires that we redistribute wealth and resources in a manner that alleviates the economic and social discrepancies discussed at the beginning of this chapter. Justice ideally knows no racial, religious, gender or national borders. But if moral cosmopolitanism is correct, it may require institutional cosmopolitanism to implement it.

The Cosmopolitan-Justice Imperative: The Possibility of World Government

Peace, justice, and the war against terrorism and violence may be won only by institutional cosmopolitanism, world government. Two arguments can be made for world government. The first one is the *Moral Point of View Argument*, which we have already discussed in this chapter. The moral point of view is impartial and universal, treating every rational being as a moral citizen. The second argument is the *Trend toward Globalism Argument*, to which I briefly adumbrate.

The world is shrinking. It is becoming a global village. In a village your neighbor's problems are, to some significant extent, your problems. If his child is delinquent, you suffer from it. If your neighbor's house is on fire, yours is threatened. Similarly, in today's world, an economic downturn in Japan, an uprising in Africa or a strike in Venezuela by oil workers affects the rest of the world economy. Environmental concerns, such as pollution control, are international matters. So are health concerns, such as pandemics like AIDS and SARS, neither of which recognizes national boundaries. Transnational corporations, which are decentralized, fluid, and interdependent, are growing in wealth and influence, creating a new nonnationalist political force in the world, which calls for legal constraints. International terrorism poses a threat to civilization. Fanatical suicide bombers are a threat to all humanity. It may require a global united CIA to intercept their nefarious activities. The geopolitics of the world has been transformed in the last decades, even before September 11, 2001. Instead of the Cold War threat of a global nuclear explosion, the trend in the past decades has been a geopolitical implosion of internecine atrocities, as the inhabitants of the former Yugoslavia revive the deadly ghosts of a former age, the Hutu engage in a genocidal slaughter of their neighbors, the Tutsi in Rwanda; Tamil rebels kill Sinhalese in the name of nationalism in Sri Lanka, Muslims battle non-Muslims in Kashmir, Lebanon, Israel, and the Baltics, while nationalist Catholic Irish engage in mutual murder with nationalist Protestants who are still fighting the Battle of the Boyne of 1690 in Northern Ireland, their nationalism trumping their common Christian heritage. The most dangerous threat to civilization are weapons of mass destruction. Chemical, biological, and nuclear weapons are more sophisticated and more accessible to more terrorist groups and rogue nations than ever before, so that a central monitoring agency will be necessary to control and coordinate measures to protect against catastrophic attacks. Furthermore, to live in peace and prosperity involves ameliorating the suffering of people in distant lands and ameliorating the dire plight of the poor, thus removing the causes of terrorism. It requires a recognition of our common humanity and, accordingly, good will in reciprocal aid for mutual advantage.

States are roughly analogous to individuals in a Hobbesian state of nature, where "life is solitary, poor, nasty, brutish, and short. . . . a war of all against all." Given nuclear weapons and the threat of terrorism, smaller nations and terrorist groups can inflict enormous damage on mighty superpowers. Just as individuals give up some liberty to the commonwealth in order to attain peace and security, the nations of the world may need to give up a degree of sovereignty in order to attain peace, security and justice in a world in which we interact in ever-closer ways. The advantages of a world government are: (1) having a central agency to maintain the peace, adjudicating between rival claims; (2) having a central agency to combat terrorism and control the spread of weapons of mass destruction; (3) having a central agency to construct and enforce international law, including devising environmental regulations necessary for health; (4) having a central agency to collect taxes and redistribute wealth to where it will do most good. Ideally, present nation-states within a World Federation would be analogous to the fifty states within the United States of America, possessing local autonomy but not absolute sovereignty. It would be a parliamentary democracy with a vertically structured, bottom-up decision-making process, so that the top tier would only come into play in adjudicating disputes unresolvable at the lower local level. From a moral point of view, there is nothing sacred about nations. If they serve humanity best, fine. Then they're justified. But if a better, more just arrangement comes along, we should adopt it.

But of course, the dangers of world government are enormous, threatening despotism on the one hand and stifling bureaucracy on the other. We don't want a *Brave New World*, nor do we desire inefficient global bureaucracy. So it is not completely obvious that justice, on balance, requires institutional cosmopolitanism. If amelioration of the world's suffering can come about through a commitment to moral cosmopolitanism in which states adhere to universal rights and international agreements, redistributing wealth in order to reduce the discrepancies between the rich and poor, well and good. But the threats to peace, welfare, and security may best be met through a central agency, such as the United Nations or a World Confederation, which is more impartial and able to enforce international law and to tax and redistribute wealth in a more just manner. The adoption of the United Nations Declaration of Universal Human Rights at the end of World War II may have been the most important moral event of the twentieth century, promoting global justice. We may need a stronger organization than the present U.N. to bring these rights to reality. If the moral advantages of institutional cosmopolitanism turn out to promote justice and utility better than our present arrangement of nation-states, the concern for justice and peace should incline us in that direction.

Conclusion

Vast discrepancies exist between rich nations and poor nations, as well as between the rich and poor within nations. The poor in many cases, through no fault of their own, are desperately needy. Individuals as well as states, artificial persons, have obligations based both on beneficence and on justice to come to the aid of the poor, to help them meet their basic needs and enable them to become self-sufficient. The principle of humanity focuses on our common features as human beings rather than on national boundaries, so that, while we have primary obligations to those who are more closely related to us, we ought to be concerned with all people everywhere. Finally, the cosmopolitan vision might lead us to world government as the best means for realizing world peace, environmental wholeness, and justice.

Notes

1. *United Nations Development Report 2000* (New York: Oxford University Press, 2000) and World Bank, *World Development Report 2002* (New York: Oxford University Press, 2002).

2. For a good discussion of these discrepancies, see Peter Singer, *One World* (New York: Oxford University Press, 2002), Chapter 5. I am indebted to Singer's work for calling my attention to these facts.

3. See U.S. Federal Budget, 2003. See also Singer, *One World*, pp. 180ff. The United Nations has set the figure of 0.7% of a nation's gross national product (GNP) as a goal for foreign aid. Only four nations meet that goal: Denmark, Sweden, Norway, and the Netherlands. Japan gives 0.22%, but the United States only 0.11%. Much of this goes to military aid.

4. One type of feminism, emphasizing *care*, should also be included in denying that we have obligations to aid the poor in other nations. A leading proponent, Nel Noddings, argues that we are not obliged to care for starving children in Africa. (Nel Noddings, *Caring: A Feminist Approach to Ethics and Moral Education* [University of California Press, 1986], p. 86). Other feminists take a cosmopolitan approach.

5. John Rawls, *A Theory of Justice* (Cambridge, MA: Harvard University Press, 1971). Rawls qualifies his earlier position in his later work, *The Laws of the People* (Cambridge, MA: Harvard University Press, 1999), arguing that states have obligations "to assist burdened societies" (p.106), but he still does not apply his *difference principle* to people outside one's state.

6. Charles R. Beitz, *Political Theory and International Relations* (Princeton, NJ: Princeton University Press, 1979), pp. 154–61.

7. Peter Unger, *Living High and Letting Die* (New York: Oxford University Press, 1996), pp. 9, 136.

8. The two best works in favor of this theory are Henry Shue, *Basic Rights: Subsistence, Affluence and U. S. Foreign Policy* (Princeton, NJ: Princeton University Press, 1996) and Charles Jones, *Global Justice* (New York: Oxford University Press, 1999).

9. Luke 10: 29–37.

10. The posterity problem haunts many ethical theories. Egoists fail to provide a solution to this problem, asking "Why should I care about posterity? What has posterity ever done for me?" Kantians, too, fail to address it, for they require rational agents as the objects of our duties, but future people aren't identifiable, for they don't exist. Consequentialist doctrines like utilitarianism seem to have the best solution: we have a duty to create general welfare, including the conditions of welfare for those not yet born.

11. I owe this counterexample to Stephen Kershnar.

12. Joel Feinberg, "The Nature and Value of Rights," *The Journal of Value Inquiry* (1970).

13. The illustration is based on Henry Shue, *Basic Rights* (Princeton, NJ: Princeton University Press, 1980), 42f. Shue writes, "The story contains no implication that the man from the capital or the peasant-turned-foreman were malicious or intended to do anything worse than single-mindedly pursue their own respective interests. But the outsider's offer of the contract was another causal factor, in producing the maldistribution that would probably persist, barring protective intervention, for at least the decade the contract was to be honored. If the families in the village had rights to subsistence, their rights were being violated. Society, acting presumably by way of the government, ought to protect them from a severe type of harm that eliminates their ability to feed themselves."

14. Amartya Sen, *Poverty and Famine* (New York: Oxford University Press, 1981).

15. My discussion here is based on that of Charles R. Beitz, *Political Theory and International Relations* (Princeton, NJ: Princeton University, 1979), pp. 137–43.

16. Charles Darwin, *The Descent of Man* (1873).

CHAPTER 8

Justice and Punishment

> What kind and what degree of punishment does public justice take as its principle and norm? None other than the principle of equality in the movement of the pointer of the scale of justice, the principle of not inclining to one side more than to the other. Thus any undeserved evil which you do to someone else among the people is an evil done to yourself. If you rob him, you rob yourself; if you slander him, you slander yourself; if you strike him, you strike yourself; and if you kill him, you kill yourself.[1]
>
> (Immanuel Kant)

Why Do We Have a System of Punishment?

While traveling toward Thebes, Oedipus encounters Laius, who provokes a fight with him. Oedipus defends himself and kills his assailant. Upon arriving in Thebes, Oedipus finds the city besieged by a plague, caused by the Sphinx, who put a riddle to each passerby, destroying those who are unable to answer it. Oedipus solved the riddle and thereby ended the plague. As a reward he is made king of Thebes and is joined in wedlock to the widowed Queen, Jocasta. Alas, unbeknownst to Oedipus, Laius, whom he had slain, was his biological father, and Jocasta, whom he has married, is his mother. Oedipus is condemned for his patricide and incest, forced to relinquish his throne, pluck out his eyes, and go into exile.

We experience revulsion over the injustice of the case of strict liability. Oedipus didn't deserve such harsh punishment; indeed, he merited no punishment at all. He didn't purposefully kill his father or marry his mother; rather he killed in self-defense an assailant, who turned out to be his biological father, and he married a woman whom he had every reason to believe was an eligible widow, not his mother. We believe that even if patricide and incest are morally wrong, Oedipus is excused of wrongdoing, for he lacked the requisite knowledge and intention to constitute blameworthiness.

Moral wrong, reflected in our criminal system, requires evil intention, *mens rea* ("a guilty mind"). As Justice Oliver Wendell Holmes quipped, even a dog knows the difference between being tripped over accidentally and being kicked on purpose. If the main purpose of the criminal law were simply deterrence, we might adopt a strict liability system (as we do regarding statutory rape—putting the burden on the man to make sure that the woman he is having sex with is an adult). But we think there is more to wrongness than simply a bad act. A necessary condition for just punishment is guilt. The criminal must deserve the punishment and deserve the type and amount of punishment applied.

To be responsible for a past act is to be liable to praise or blame. If the act was especially good, we go further than praise; we reward it. If it was especially evil, we go further than blame; we punish it. In order to examine the notion of punishment, we first need to inquire under what conditions, if any, criminal punishment is justified. We will examine three approaches to this problem: the retributivist, the utilitarian, and the rehabilitationist.

Even though few of us will ever become criminals or be indicted on criminal charges, most of us harbor deep feelings about the matter of criminal punishment. Something about crime touches the deepest nerves of our imagination. Take the following situations, which are based on newspaper reports from the mid-1990s:

1. A sex pervert lures little children into his home, sexually abuses them, and then kills them. Over twenty bodies are discovered on his property.
2. A man sends his wife and daughter on an airplane trip and puts a time bomb into their luggage, having taken out a million dollar insurance policy on their lives. The money will be used to pay off his gambling debts and for prostitutes. (Fortunately, the bomb failed to detonate, and the culprit was apprehended.)
3. Note these descriptions by Mike Royko:

> The small crowd that gathered outside the prison to protest the execution of Steven Judy softly sang, 'We Shall Overcome.'. . . But it didn't seem quite the same hearing it sung out of concern for someone who, on finding a woman with a flat tire, raped and murdered her and drowned her three small children, then said that he hadn't been 'losing any sleep' over his crimes. . . .
>
> I remember the grocer's wife. She was a plump, happy woman who enjoyed the long workday she shared with her husband in their ma-and-pa store. One evening, two young men came in and showed guns, and the grocer gave them everything in the cash register.
>
> For no reason, almost as an afterthought, one of the men shot the grocer in the face. The woman stood only a few feet from her husband when he was turned into a dead, bloody mess.
>
> She was about 50 when it happened. In a few years her mind was almost gone, and she looked 80. They might as well have killed her too.
>
> Then there was the woman I got to know after her daughter was killed by a wolfpack gang during a motoring trip. The mother called me occasionally, but nothing that I said could ease her torment. It ended when she took her own life. . . .
>
> A couple of years ago I spent a long evening with the husband, sister and parents of a fine young woman who had been forced into the trunk of a car in a hospital parking lot. The degenerate who kidnapped her kept her in the trunk, like an ant in a jar, until he got tired of the game. Then he killed her.[2]

What is it within us that rises up in indignation at the thought of these evil deeds? What should happen to the criminals in these cases? How can the victims (or their loved ones) ever be compensated for these crimes? We feel conflicting emotional judgments of harsh vengeance toward the criminal and, at the same time, concern that we don't ourselves become violent and irrational in our quest for just punishment. But what exactly is justice in punishment?

The Definition of Punishment

We may define "punishment," or more precisely "institutional or legal punishment," as an *evil inflicted by a person in a position of authority upon another person who is judged to have violated a rule*.[3] It can be analyzed into five concepts:

1. *An evil:* To punish is to inflict harm, unpleasantness, or suffering (not necessarily pain). Regarding this concept, the question is: Under what conditions is it right to cause harm or inflict suffering?
2. *For a violation of a rule:* The violation is either a moral or a legal offense. The pertinent questions are: Should we punish everyone who commits a moral offense? Need the offense already have been committed, or may we engage in prophylactic punishment where we have good evidence that the agent will commit a crime?
3. *Done to the offender:* The offender must be judged or believed to be guilty of a crime. Does this rule out the possibility of punishing innocent people? What should we call the process of "framing" the innocent and "punishing" them?
4. *Carried out by a personal agency:* The punisher must be a rational agent, rather than a natural phenomenon, such as an earthquake or disease.
5. *Imposed by an authority:* The agent who punishes must be justified in carrying out the evil.

Let us spend a moment examining each of these points and the questions they raise.

1. Punishment is an evil. It may involve corporal punishment, loss of rights or freedom, or even loss of life. These are things we normally condemn as immoral. How does what is normally considered morally wrong suddenly become morally right? To quote H. L. A. Hart, former Oxford University professor of jurisprudence, What is this "mysterious piece of moral alchemy in which the combination of two evils of moral wickedness and suffering are transmuted into good"?[4] Theories of punishment bear the burden of proof to justify why punishment is morally required. The three classical theories have been retribution, deterrence, and rehabilitation, which we shall examine below. These theories attempt not only to justify types of punishment, but also to provide guidance on the degrees of punishment to be given for various crimes and persons.

2. Punishment is administered for an offense, but must it be for a violation of a legal statute, or may it also be for any moral failure? Although most legal scholars

agree that the law should have a moral basis, it is impractical to make laws against every moral wrong. If we had a law against lying, for example, our courts would become cluttered beyond their ability to function. Also, some laws may be immoral (e.g., anti-abortionists believe that the laws permitting abortion are immoral), but they still are laws, carrying with them coercive measures.

Whether we should punish only offenses already committed or also crimes that are intended is a difficult question. If I know or have good evidence that Smith is about to kill some innocent child (but not which one), and the only way to prevent this is by incarcerating Smith (or killing him), why isn't this morally acceptable? Normally, we don't have certainty about people's intentions, so we can't be certain that Smith really means to kill the child. But what if we do have strong evidence in this case? Nations sometimes launch preemptive strikes when they have strong evidence of an impending attack (e.g., Israel in the Six-Day War in 1967 acted on reliable information that Arab nations were going to attack it. It launched a preemptive strike that probably saved many Israeli lives). Although preemptive strikes are about defense, not punishment per se, could the analogy carry over? After all, part of the role of punishment is defense against future crimes.

3. Punishment is done to the offender. No criminologist justifies punishing the innocent, but classic cases of framing the innocent in order to maximize utility exist. Sometimes Caiaphas's decision to frame and execute Jesus of Nazareth (John 10:50) is cited. "It were better that one man should die for a nation than that the whole nation perish." Utilitarians seem to be especially vulnerable to such practices, but every utilitarian philosopher of law eschews such egregious miscarriages of justice. Why this is so is a point I will discuss below.

This stipulation, "done to an offender," also rules out other uses of the word "punish," as when, for instance, we say that boxer Mike Tyson "punished" his opponent with a devastating left to the jaw. Such metaphorical or nonlegal uses of the term are excluded from our analysis. Similarly, although the law allows for the quarantine of confirmed or potential disease carriers, we would not call this imposed suffering "punishment." The reason is that our intention is not to cause suffering but to prevent it, and the carrier is understood to be innocent of any wrongdoing.

4. Punishment is carried out by a personal agency. Punishment is not the work of natural forces but of people. Lightning may strike and kill a criminal, but only people (or conscious beings) can punish other people.

5. Punishment is imposed by an authority. Punishment is conferred through institutions that have to do with maintaining laws or social codes. This rules out vigilante executions as punishments. Only a recognized authority, such as the state, can carry out legal punishment for criminal behavior. More controversially, it rules out *poetic justice*, as happens when events conspire to cause the wrongdoer the harm that the law should impose. For example, in Charles Dickens's *Oliver Twist*, the murderer Bill Sykes, in fleeing the police, loses his footing on a steep roof whereupon the rope he is using to rappel downwards slips, enclosing his neck and hanging him from the rooftop.

We turn now to the leading theories on punishment.

Theories of Punishment

Retributivist Theories

Retributivist theories make infliction of punishment dependent upon what the agent, as a wrongdoer, deserves, rather than upon any future social utility that might result from the infliction of suffering on the criminal. That is, rather than focusing on any future good that might result from punishment, retributivist theories are *backward* looking, assessing the nature of the misdeed. The most forceful proponents of this view are Immanuel Kant (1724–1804), C. S. Lewis (1898–1963), and Herbert Morris. Here is a classic quotation from Kant, which deserves to be quoted at length:

> Juridical punishment can never be administered merely as a means for promoting another good either with regard to the criminal himself or to civil society, but must in all cases be imposed only because the individual on whom it is inflicted *has committed a crime*. For one man ought never to be dealt with merely as a means subservient to the purpose of another, nor be mixed up with the subjects of real right. Against such treatment his inborn personality has a right to protect him, even though he may be condemned to lose his civil personality. He must first be found guilty and *punishable* before there can be any thought of drawing from his punishment any benefit for himself or his fellow-citizens.
>
> The principle of punishment is a categorical imperative, and woe to him who creeps through the serpent-windings of utilitarianism to discover some advantage that may discharge him from the justice of punishment, or even reduces its amount by the advantage it promises, in accordance with the Pharisaical maxim, "It is better for *one* man to die than for an entire people to perish" [John 10:51]. For if justice and righteousness perish, there is no longer any value in men's living on the earth.
>
> But what kind and what amount of punishment is it that public justice makes its principle and standard? It is the principle of equality, by which the pointer of the scale of justice is made to incline no more to the one side than the other. It may be rendered by saying that the undeserved evil which any one commits on another, is to be regarded as perpetrated on himself. Hence it may be said, "If you slander another, you slander yourself; if you steal from another you steal from yourself; if you strike another, you strike yourself; if you kill another, you kill yourself." This is the *law of retribution (jus talionis)*— it being understood, of course, that this is applied by a court as distinguished from private judgment. It is the only principle that can definitely assign both the quality and the quantity of a just penalty. All other standards are wavering and uncertain; and on account of other considerations involved in them, they contain no principle conformable to the sentence of pure and strict justice.[5]

This is a classic expression of the retributivist position, *the Strict Equality Argument*, for it bases punishment solely on the issue of whether or not the subject in question has committed a crime and punishes him accordingly. All other considerations—eudaimonistic or "serpent-windings of utilitarianism"—are rejected as irrelevant. For example, Kant considers the possibility of a capital criminal allowing himself to be a subject in a medical experiment as a substitute for capital punishment in order to benefit the society, but he rejects the suggestion. "A court would reject with contempt such a proposal from a medical college, for justice ceases to be justice if it can be bought for any price whatsoever."

Kant and the classic retributivist position in general have three theses about the justification of punishment:

1. Guilt is a necessary condition for judicial punishment; that is, *only* the guilty may be punished.
2. Guilt is a sufficient condition for judicial punishment; that is, *all* the guilty must be punished. If you have committed a crime, morality demands that you suffer an evil for it.
3. The correct amount of punishment imposed upon the morally (or legally) guilty offender is that amount which is *equal* to the moral seriousness of the offense.

There are various ways of arguing for these theses. One is to argue, as Kant does, that in lying, stealing, unjustly striking, or killing another, the offender lies, steals, unjustly strikes or kills himself. That is, by universalizing the maxim of such acts, the offender wills a like action on himself. This is the law of retaliation (*jus talionis*). "The undeserved evil which anyone commits on another is to be regarded as perpetuated on himself." The criminal need not consciously desire the same punishment, but by acting on such a principle, for example, "murder your enemies," the offender implicitly draws the same treatment on himself. He deserves to suffer in the same way he has harmed another. Or, at least, the suffering should be equal and similar to the suffering he has caused. This is the *strict equality* (sometimes called the *"lex talionis"*) interpretation of retributivism.

The weakness of the *Strict Equality* interpretation is that it is both impractical and impossible to inflict the very same kind of suffering on the offender as he has imposed on others. Our social institutions are not equipped to measure the exact amount of harm done by offenders or repay them in kind. We rightly shrink from torturing the torturer or resuscitating the serial murderer so that we can "kill" him a second, a third, a fourth time, and so forth. How do you give a trusted member of the FBI or CIA who betrays his country by spying for the enemy an equivalent harm? Our legal systems are not equipped to punish according to the harm inflicted but, rather, according to the wrong done, measured against specified statutes with prescribed penalties.

A second way, following Herbert Morris and Michael Davis's *Fair Play Argument*, is to interpret these theses in terms of social equilibrium.[6] The criminal has violated a mutually beneficial scheme of social cooperation, thereby treating law-abiding members of the community unfairly. Punishment restores the scales of justice, the social equilibrium of benefits and burdens. We might put the argument this way.

1. In breaking a primary rule of society, a person obtains an unfair advantage over others.
2. Unfair advantages ought to be redressed by society if possible.
3. Punishment is a form of redressing the unfair advantage.
4. Therefore, we ought to punish the offender for breaking the primary rule.

Punishment restores the social equilibrium of burdens and benefits by taking from the agent what he or she unfairly got and now owes, that is, exacting his or her debt. This argument, like the Kantian one above, holds that society has a duty to punish the offender, since society has a general duty to redress "unfair advantages . . . if possible." That is, we have a prima facie duty to eliminate unfair advantages in society, even though that duty may be overridden by other considerations such as the high cost (financially or socially) of doing so or the criminal's repentance.

Although the Kantian interpretation focuses on the nature and gravity of the harm done by the offender, Morris's *Fair Play Argument* focuses on the unfairness of the offense—the idea of unfair advantage that ought to be repaid to society. Although it is not always the case that the criminal gains an advantage or profit from crime, he or she does abandon the common burden of self-restraint in order to obtain criminal ends. While the rest of us are forgoing the use of unlawful and immoral means to obtain our goals, while we are restraining ourselves from taking these kinds of shortcuts, the criminal makes use of these means to his or her ends. As such we have been unfairly taken advantage of, and justice requires the annulment of the unfair advantage. The criminal must repay his or her debt to society. He or she need not be punished in the same way as his or her offense, but the punishment must "fit the crime," be a proportionate response.

It is not clear, however, that Morris's and Davis's interpretation can do all the work. For one thing it is modeled on the act of stealing (or cheating), getting an unfair advantage over others. The criminal may obtain an unfair advantage over others by cheating on exams or taxes, by killing a rival for a job, or by stealing another's purse, but this model of unfair advantage doesn't work as well with sadistic crimes that may leave the criminal psychologically worse off than the victim. The successful rapist may be worse off, not better off, than before his crime. The terrorist who detonates a bomb on the crowded bus he is riding doesn't gain any advantage over others, for he no longer exists. Furthermore, we do not punish all instances of unfair advantage, as when someone lies. Daniel Farrell has objected to the *Fair Play Argument*, pointing out that even before we enter into a social contract, even in a Lockean state of nature, the concept of just desert holds, and we should intervene on behalf of an innocent victim who is being attacked by an aggressor, a malicious rapist or a killer.[7] Moreover, we think someone is deserving of punishment even when he only *attempts*—with malice aforethought (*mens rea*)—to harm others, when his intention to do evil is unsuccessful.

Let us turn to the third thesis of the retributivist argument:

The correct amount of punishment imposed upon the morally (or legally) guilty offender is that amount which is *equal* to the moral seriousness of the offense.

Determining exactly what is the right amount and type of punishment is a controversial issue for retributivists. Some punishments, such as torture or rape, seem to be violations of our human dignity, terrible reductions of our humanity to the subhuman. Kant thought that rapists should be castrated and those engaging in beastiality banished. Thomas Jefferson supported such a system of proportionality of punishment to crime:

Whosoever shall be guilty of rape, polygamy, sodomy with man or woman, shall be punished, if a man, by castration, if a woman by cutting through the cartilage of her nose a hole of one half inch in diameter at the least. [And] whosoever shall maim another, or shall disfigure him . . . shall be maimed, or disfigured in the like sort: or if that cannot be, for want of some part, then as nearly as may be, in some other part of at least equal value.

The notion of proportionality brings us back to our concept of desert.

Desert and Retributive Justice

Both the *Strict Equality* (*lex talionis*) and the *Fair Play* interpretations of retributivism have some validity, but both partially misfire. Strict Equality of punishment is not practical or necessary for retributive justice. On the other hand, the Fair Play argument overemphasizes the advantage gained by the criminal, fails to account for evil intentions, *mens rea*, and tends to treat punishment as restitution. But both theories correctly point to the broader, underlying ground for punishment: that the criminal deserves suffering in a way fitting his or her crime. Farrell correctly points to this salient feature—*desert*, which exists even in a Lockean state of nature (a precontractual state). While it is not practical, let alone necessary, to punish the criminal in a manner equal to the gravity of the crime, we can punish him or her in a manner proportionate to the seriousness of the offense. We should construct two columns, one ranking crimes according to their seriousness and the other ranking punishments according to their severity, and then we should match the type of crime with the appropriate type of punishment. So we should modify the third premise of the Strict Equality interpretation to read:

The correct amount of punishment imposed upon the morally (or legally) guilty offender is that amount which is proportionate to the moral seriousness of the offense.

The concept of desert is connected with our notion of responsibility. As free agents who can choose, a moral universe would be so arranged that we would be rewarded or punished in a manner equal to our virtue or vice. As the ancient adage puts it, "Whatsoever a man sows that shall he also reap." Those who sow good deeds would reap good results, and those who choose to sow their wild oats would reap accordingly. Given a notion of objective morality, the good should prosper and the evil should suffer—both in equal measure to their virtue or vice. This idea is reflected in the Eastern idea of karma: You will be repaid in the next life for what you did in this one. The ancient Greek philosophers and the Roman jurists, beginning with Cicero, define justice as giving to each his due, *suum cuique tribuens*. Jesus may be seen as adumbrating the same principle in his statement, "Render unto Caesar that which is Caesar's and unto God that which is God's" (Luke 20:25). In the Christian tradition it is reflected in the doctrine of heaven and hell (and purgatory). The good will be rewarded according to their good works, and the evil will be punished in hell—which they have chosen by their actions.

It would seem that eternal hell is excessive punishment for human evil and eternal bliss excessive reward, but the basic idea of *moral fittingness* seems to make sense. G. W. Leibniz refers to the same principle that Kant, as noted above, calls the principle of *equality*, a sort of symmetry between input and output in any endeavor. We get a hint of this symmetry in the practice of gratitude. We normally and spontaneously feel grateful for services rendered. Someone treats us to dinner, gives us a present, teaches us a skill, rescues us from a potential disaster or simply gives us directions. A sense of gratitude wells up inside of us toward our benefactor; we feel indebted, and sense that we have a duty to reciprocate in kind. On the other hand, if someone intentionally and cruelly hurts us, deceives us, betrays our trust, we feel involuntary resentment. We want to reciprocate and harm that person. The offender deserves to be harmed, and we have a right to harm him. If he has harmed someone else, we have an instinctual duty to harm him. Henry Sidgwick argued that these basic emotions are in fact the grounds for our notion of desert: Punishment is resentment universalized and rewards—a sort of positive retribution—gratitude universalized.[8] Whether such a reduction of desert to resentment and gratitude completely explains our notion of desert may be questioned, but it lends support to two theses: first, that there is natural, preinstitutional desert and, second, that desert creates obligations.

Retributive theories of justice focus on human dignity. Human beings are self-conscious moral agents able to act responsibly. It is precisely their capacity for moral responsibility that bestows dignity and a right to life on them. Intentionally taking the life of an innocent human being is so evil that the perpetrator forfeits his own right to life. He or she deserves to die.

Criminals like Steven Judy, Timothy McVeigh, Ted Bundy (who is reported to have raped and murdered over 100 women), and John Allen Muhammed and Lee Malvo, the two snipers who gunned down thirteen people in Maryland and Virginia in November 2002, have committed capital offenses and deserve nothing less than capital punishment. No doubt malicious acts like the ones committed by these criminals deserve worse punishment than death, but if retributivism is true, the death penalty may well be warranted.

Let me finally clear up one misunderstanding. People often confuse *retribution* with *revenge*. While moral people will feel outrage at acts of heinous crimes, such as those mentioned above, the moral justification of punishment is not *vengeance* but *desert*. Vengeance signifies inflicting harm on the offender out of anger because of what he has done. Retribution is the rationally supported theory that the criminal deserves a punishment fitting to the gravity of his crime.

The nineteenth-century British philosopher James Fitzjames Stephens thought vengeance was a justification for punishment, arguing that punishment should be inflicted "for the sake of ratifying the feeling of hatred—call it revenge, resentment, or what you will—which the contemplation of such [offensive] conduct excites in healthily constituted minds."[9] But retributivism is not based on hatred for the criminal (though a feeling of vengeance may accompany the punishment). Retributivism is the theory that the criminal *deserves* to be punished and deserves to be punished in proportion to the gravity of his or her crime—whether or not the victim or anyone else desires it. We may all deeply regret having to carry out the punishment but consider it warranted.

On the other hand, people do have a sense of outrage and passion for revenge at criminals for their crimes. Stephens was correct in asserting that "[t]he criminal law stands to the passion for revenge in much the same relation as marriage to the sexual appetite."[10] Failure to punish would no more lessen our sense of vengeance than the elimination of marriage would lessen our sexual appetite. When a society fails to punish criminals in a way thought to be proportionate to the gravity of the crime, the danger arises that the public would take the law into its own hands, resulting in vigilante justice, lynch mobs, and private acts of retribution. The outcome is likely to be an anarchistic, insecure state of injustice. As such, legal retribution stands as a safeguard for an orderly application of punitive desert.

Our natural instinct is for *vengeance*, but civilization demands that we restrain our anger and go through a legal process, letting the outcome determine whether and to what degree to punish the accused. Civilization demands that we not take the law into our own hands, but it should also satisfy our deepest instincts when they are consonant with reason. Our instincts tell us that some crimes, like McVeigh's, Judy's and Bundy's, should be severely punished, but we refrain from personally carrying out those punishments, committing ourselves to the legal processes. The death penalty is supported by our gut animal instincts as well as our sense of justice as desert.

The death penalty reminds us that there are consequences to our actions, that we are responsible for what we do, so that dire consequences for immoral actions are eminently appropriate.[11] The death penalty is such a fitting response to evil.

Deterrence

Utilitarian theories are theories of deterrence, reform, and prevention. The emphasis is not on the gravity of the evil done, but on deterring and preventing future evil. Their motto might be, "Don't cry over spilt milk!" Unlike retributive theories, which are backward-looking and based on desert, utilitarian theories are *forward*-looking, based on social improvement. Jeremy Bentham (1748–1832) and John Stuart Mill (1806–1873) are classic utilitarians. Their position can be analyzed into three theses:

1. Social utility (including reform, prevention, and deterrence) is a necessary condition for judicial punishment.
2. Social utility is a sufficient condition for judicial punishment.
3. The proper amount of punishment to be imposed upon the offender is that amount which will do the most good (or least harm) to all those who will be affected by it. Stanley Benn puts it well: "The margin of increment of harm inflicted on the offender should be preferable to the harm avoided by fixing that penalty rather than one slightly lower."[12]

Punishment is a technique of social control, justified as long as it prevents more evil than it produces. If there is a system of social control that will give a greater balance (e.g., rehabilitation), then the utilitarian will opt for that. The utilitarian doesn't accept Draconian laws that would deter because the punishment would be worse than the crime, causing greater suffering than the original offense. Only three grounds are permissible for meting out punishment: (1) to prevent a repetition; (2) to deter others—the threat of punishment deters potential offenders; and (3) to rehabilitate the criminal (this need not be seen as punishment, but it may involve that).

The threat of punishment is everything. Every act of punishment is to that extent an admission of the failure of the threat. If the threat were successful, no punishment would be needed, and the question of justification would not arise.

One problem with the utilitarian theory is simply that it goes against our notion of desert. It says that social utility is a necessary condition for punishment. But I would be in favor of punishing at least the most egregious offenders even if I knew they would never commit another crime. Suppose we discovered Adolf Hitler living quietly in a small Argentine town and were sure that no good (in terms of deterrence or prevention) would come of punishing him. Shouldn't we still bring him to trial and punish him appropriately?

A further problem is that utilitarianism would seem to enjoin punishment for prospective crimes. If the best evidence we have leads us to believe that some person or group of people will commit a crime, we are justified in applying punitive measures if our actions satisfy a cost-benefit analysis.

The main weakness of utilitarianism is that it seems to allow the punishment of the innocent if that will deter others from crime. We want only criminals punished, but utilitarians focus on results, not justice. If we can frame an innocent bum for a rape and murder in order to prevent a riot, the utilitarian will be tempted to do so. This violates the essence of justice.

Some philosophers, namely, Anthony Quinton, Stanley Benn, and R. S. Peters, have rejected this criticism as missing the point of what punishment is. They contend that punishment is logically connected with committing a crime, so that the one punished must be presumed guilty.[13] But this "definitional stop" only moves the problem to a different dimension without solving it. Suppose we call "punishment" punishing the guilty and give another name, such as "telishment" (Rawls's suggestion), to judicially harming the innocent for deterrent purposes. Now the question becomes "Should we ever telish people?" The utilitarian is committed to telishment—whenever the aggregate utility warrants it.

Although these criticisms are severe, they do not overthrow utilitarianism altogether. One surely admits that penal law should have a deterrent effect. The point seems to be that utilitarian theories need a retributive base on which to build. I will comment on this point later.

Rehabilitative Theories

In Samuel Butler's satirical Victorian novel *Erewhon* (1862), sick people are punished with prison sentences in proportion to the gravity of their "crime," and those who break the law, murderers and thieves, are confined to hospitals until they are "cured." Butler is mocking our institutional arrangements, but part of his satire expresses a modern critique of criminal punishment. According to rehabilitative theories, crime is a disease, and the criminal is a sick person who needs to be cured, not punished. Such rehabilitationists as B. F. Skinner, Karl Menninger, and Benjamin Karpman point to the failures and cruelties of our penal system and advocate an alternative of therapy and reconditioning. "Therapy, not torture" might be said to be their motto, for criminals are not really in control of their behavior but are suffering from personality disorders. Crime is by and large a result of an adverse early environment, so that what must be done is to recondition the criminal through positive reinforcement. Punishment is a prescientific response to antisocial behavior. At best punishment temporarily suppresses adverse behavior, but, if untreated, Skinner argues, it will resurface again as though the punishment never occurred. It is useless as a deterrent. Rehabilitationists charge that retributivists are guilty of holding an antiquated notion of human beings as possessing free wills and being responsible for their behavior. We, including all of our behavior, are products of our heredity and, especially, our environment.

Menninger sees rehabilitation as a replacement for the concept of justice in criminal procedure:

> The very word *justice* irritates scientists. No surgeon expects to be asked if an operation for cancer is just or not. No doctor will be reproached on the grounds that the dose of penicillin he has prescribed is less or more than *justice* would stipulate. . . . It does not advance a solution to use the word *justice*. It is a subjective emotional word. . . . the concept is so vague, so distorted in its application, so hypocritical, and usually so irrelevant that it offers no help in the solution of the crime problem which it exists to combat but results in its exact opposite—injustice, injustice to everybody.[14]

We need to confine criminals for their own good and society's, but a process of positive reinforcement must be the means of dealing with criminals and their "crimes." Benjamin Karpman, one of the proponents of this theory, puts it this way:

> Basically, criminality is but a symptom of insanity, using the term in its widest generic sense to express unacceptable social behavior based on unconscious motivation flowing from a disturbed instinctive and emotional life, whether this appears in frank psychoses, or in less obvious form in neuroses and unrecognized psychoses. . . . If criminals are products of early environmental influences in the same sense that psychotics and neurotics are, then it should be possible to reach them psychotherapeutically.[15]

Let me begin my criticism of the rehabilitation theory by relating a retelling of the Good Samaritan story (Luke 10). You'll recall that a man went down from Jerusalem to Jericho and fell among thieves who beat him, robbed him, and left him for dead. A priest and a Levite passed him by, but an outcast Samaritan came to the beaten man's rescue, bringing him to a hotel for treatment and paying the bills for his care.

A contemporary version of the story goes like this. A man is brutally robbed and left on the side of the road by his assailants. A priest comes by but regrets having to leave the man in his condition, in order to avoid being late for the church service he must lead. Similarly, a lawyer passes by, rushing to meet a client. Finally, a psychiatrist sees our subject, rushes over to him, places the man's head in his lap and in a distraught voice cries out, "Oh, this is awful! How deplorable! Tell me, Sir, who did this to you. He needs help."

Not all psychiatrists fit this description of mislocating the victim, but the story cannot be dismissed as merely a joke in poor taste. It fits an attitude that substitutes the concept of sickness for moral failure. Let me briefly note some of the problems with the whole theory of rehabilitation as a substitute for punishment. First, this doctrine undermines the very notion of human autonomy and responsibility. Individuals who are not mentally ill are free agents whose actions should be taken seriously as flowing from free decisions. If a person kills in cold blood, he or she must bear the responsibility for that murder. Rehabilitation theories reduce moral problems to medical problems.

Furthermore, rehabilitation doesn't seem to work. Rehabilitation is a form of socialization through sophisticated medical treatment. Although humans are malleable, there are limits to what socialization and medical technology can do. Socialization can be relatively effective in infancy and early childhood, less so in late childhood, but even less effective in adulthood. Perhaps at some future time when brain manipulation becomes possible, we will make greater strides toward behavior modification, even being able to plant electrodes in a criminal's brain and so affect his cerebral cortex that he "repents" of his crime and is restored to society. The question then will be whether we have a right to tamper with someone's psyche in this manner. Furthermore, would a neurologically induced repentance for a crime really be repentance—or would it be an overriding of the criminal's autonomy and personality? And won't that tampering itself be a form of punishment?

Application to the Death Penalty

Probably the most controversial aspect of punishment revolves around the issue of the death penalty or capital punishment. Retentionists, who seek to retain the institution of capital punishment, argue that it is justified on the basis of either retributivism or deterrence. Abolitionists, who seek to abolish the institution, claim that the death penalty does not deter and is not necessary for retributive justice. A long prison sentence would do as well. They may also add that our judicial system is vulnerable to error and prejudice, so that a disproportionate number of minority members and some innocent people are executed, while the rich can hire the best lawyers to escape the electric chair. Although this is not the place to definitively decide the matter, it should be briefly discussed and the relevant issues clarified.[16]

One can separate the theoretical from the practical issue of capital punishment. On the theoretical side, we must ask whether the death penalty is ever morally permissible. Do murderers like Timothy McVeigh and Ted Bundy, who is reported to have raped and murdered over a hundred women, deserve to be executed by the state? If we review the nature of retributive justice, it is likely we will conclude that such cold-blooded murder deserves capital punishment. But if life in prison turns out to be just as effective, retributivism may not decide the issue one way or the other.

The crucial issue may turn out to be utilitarian, depending on whether we have evidence that capital punishment does or does not deter would-be murderers from killing other people. Sometimes students argue that the evidence proves that the death penalty does not deter, but this is incorrect. The statistical evidence is ambiguous and does not prove either that capital punishment does or does not deter would-be murders. Ernest van den Haag has devised a *Best-Bet Argument* in which, in the light of insufficient evidence, we bet the lives of the guilty against the death of future victims. If we execute convicted murders, and the lives of innocent are saved, we win the bet. If we execute the murderers and the innocent are not saved, we lose the bet (and unnecessary lives are lost—the murderers). Van den Haag argues that it is better to risk the lives of the murderers than the innocent, and by not betting on the death penalty, we are negatively responsible for the loss of innocent lives just in case the death penalty does deter murder. In principle, executions would have the potential to deter murder. We can imagine a situation where the death penalty did deter rational agents bent on murder. Imagine that every time someone intentionally killed an innocent person he or she was immediately struck down by lightning. When Ted Bundy slashed the throat of the girl he and his confederates just raped, lightning struck Ted. His companions witnessing his corpse would doubtless think twice before they duplicated Ted's act. When burglar Bob pulls out his pistol and shoots bank teller Betty through her heart, lightning levels Bob in the midst of his fellow robbers and the bystanders. Do you think that the evidence of cosmic retribution would go unheeded?

Of course, we do not have such swift and sure retributivism, but the question is, whether we could improve our penal system to approximate it to a sufficient degree to justify use of the death penalty. Can we sometimes have sufficient evidence to apply the death penalty for a murder, say in the cases of McVeigh and Bundy, and apply it in a public manner that causes prospective murderers to refrain from murdering innocent people? The issue is difficult, but the movement against the use of the death penalty may be an unwarranted defeatist decision, a failure of faith in our system of criminal justice.

As I write this chapter, Governor George Ryan of Illinois has just commuted the sentences of 167 death row inmates. Apparently, some of those convicted were convicted on insufficient evidence. If so, their sentences should have been commuted and the prisoners compensated. Such decisions should be done on a case-by-case basis. If capital punishment is justified, its application should be confined to clear cases in which the guilt of the criminal is "beyond reasonable doubt." But to overthrow the whole system because of a few possible miscarriages is as unwarranted as it is a loss of faith in our system of criminal justice. No one would abolish the use of fire engines and ambulances because occasionally they kill innocent pedestrians while carrying out their mission.

Abolitionists often complain that only the poor get death sentences for murder. If their trials are fair, then they deserve the death penalty, but rich murderers may be equally deserving. At the moment, only first-degree murder and treason are crimes deemed worthy of the death penalty. Perhaps our notion of treason should be expanded to include those who betray the trust of the public, corporation executives who have the trust of ordinary people, but who, through selfish and dishonest practices, ruin their lives. My proposal is to broaden, not narrow, the scope of capital punishment, to include businessmen and women who unfairly harm the public. The executives in the recent corporation scandals who bailed out with millions of dollars while they destroyed the pension plans of thousands of employees may deserve severe punishment, and if convicted, they should receive what they deserve. My educated guess is that the threat of the death sentence would have a deterrent effect here. Whether it is feasible to apply the death penalty for horrendous white collar crimes is debatable. But there is something to be said in its favor. It would remove the impression that only the poor get executed.

Conclusion

All three theories of punishment contain elements of truth. Rehabilitationism, insofar as it seeks to restore the criminal to society as a morally whole being, has merit as an aspect of the penal process, but it cannot stand alone. Retributivism is surely correct to make guilt a necessary condition for punishment and to seek to make the punishment fit the crime. Its emphasis on desert is vital to our theory of rewards and punishment, and with this it respects humans as rational, responsible agents, who should be treated in a manner fitting to their deserts. But it may be too rigid in its *retrospective* gaze and may need mercy and a *prospective* vision. Utilitarianism seems correct in emphasizing this prospective feature of treatment with the goal of promoting human flourishing. But it is in danger of manipulating people for the social good—even of punishing the innocent or punishing the guilty more than they deserve (to serve a social purpose). John Rawls, in his classic essay, "Two Concepts of Rules," suggests one way of combining retributivism and utilitarianism. In this work he attempts to do justice to both the retributive and the utilitarian theories of punishment.[17] He maintains that there is a difference between justifying an institution and justifying a given instance where the institution is applied. The question "Why do we have law or system?" is of a different nature from the question "Why are we applying the law in the present situation in this mode?" Applied to punishment: (1) "Why do we have a system of punishment?" and (2) "Why are we harming John for his misdeed?" are two different sorts of questions. When we justify the institution of punishment, we resort to utilitarian or consequentialist considerations: A society in which the wicked prosper will offer inadequate inducement to virtue. A society in which some rules are made and enforced will get on better than a society in which no rules exist or are enforced. But when we seek to justify an individual application of punishment, we resort to retributivist considerations; for example, when someone commits a breach against the law that person merits a fitting punishment.

We can operate on two levels. On the second-order (reflective) level we accept rule utilitarianism and acknowledge that the penal law should serve society's overall good. In order to do this we need a retributive system—one that adheres to common ideas of fair play and desert. So rule utilitarianism on the second-order level yields retributivism on the first order level. As we have noted, some have interpreted this process to entail that there is no preinstitutional or natural desert or justice, but that these things only come into being by social choice. It is more accurate to say that there is a primordial or deontological idea of desert that needs social choice to become activated or institutionalized for human purposes. It is not as though society could rationally choose some other practice, but that, if it is to choose rationally—to promote its goals of flourishing and resolving conflicts of interest—it must choose to reward and punish according to one's desert.

If, as has been argued, desert is a necessary (and possibly a sufficient) condition for just punishment, this has important implications for justice altogether. That is, a symmetrical relationship seems to exist between negative and positive desert. Let us examine this thesis more closely.

The most basic form of positive desert is approval or praising, and the most basic negative form is blaming or disapproval. We praise people for what we perceive to be their good deeds, and we blame them for their bad deeds. We praise Sarah for giving hours of time to tutoring poor children or feeding the indigent. We blame Sam for shirking his responsibility to provide for his children when he gambled away his weeks' earnings at the local casino. Rewards and punishments are extensions of this basic desert behavior. When the activity reaches a threshold of social seriousness, we not only praise or blame the behavior, but reward and punish it. When Sarah's aid to the poor is perceived to be of sufficient worth, we may grant her special recognition as Citizen of the Year. When Bill excels at producing widgets, we increase his salary. When he excels in leadership, we promote him to manager. When a soldier engages in heroic action, we grant him a medal of honor. Conversely, when Bill fails to spend time with his family, we blame him for negligence. When Sam commits a crime, we do not simply blame him, but try him as a criminal and, if he is found guilty, we sentence him to an appropriate punishment. We may call this symmetry relationship the karmic principle (in line with the Hindu-Buddhist principle that as we sow, so shall we reap—except my principle is completely secular and based on morality, not religion or an afterlife).[18] Ideally, the virtuous should be happy in proportion to their virtuousness and the evil should be unhappy in proportion to their viciousness. Moral virtue is the decisive criterion in determining what a person deserves.

Whereas the karmic principle is an ideal, we acknowledge our fallibility by being more circumspect in applying negative than positive desert. It is worse to do evil than to fail to do good. It is worse to mistakenly punish someone for an alleged crime than to mistakenly reward him for an alleged good deed. We commit a greater injustice in infringing the liberty of a person in punishing him or her than we do in rewarding someone. We acknowledge this in the maxim that it is better to let ten guilty men go free than to punish one innocent man. (Actually, this maxim is an exaggeration, but the point is well-made that it is a tragedy to punish the innocent person for a crime he or she didn't commit. So, we presume the accused to be innocent until proven guilty. The greater the crime involved, the greater the need for fairness and compelling evidence in order to overturn the presumption of innocence. On the other hand, we do not normally require same level of scrutiny in rewarding people for their good deeds.

In both rewarding and punishing on the basis of desert, intention is a necessary condition for the attribution of the desert, though it is of more importance regarding punishment. If Sam accidentally or unintentionally discovers the cure for cancer or rescues a kidnapped child, it is of no great moment if we reward him for his luck; but if Sid didn't intentionally kill Sarah, but only accidentally caused her death, we alter the charge from first-degree murder to involuntary manslaughter, a charge warranting a lesser punishment than murder. Similarly, if we find that the person in question is severely retarded or brain damaged, so that he didn't know what he was doing, we are likely to drop the charge of guilt but less likely to withdraw the reward.

We can represent our thesis in the form of a chart:

Positive	Negative
Approval	Disapproval
Praise	Blame
Reward	Punishment

Our actual practices of rewarding and punishing have also secondary consequentialist purposes of encouraging good behavior and discouraging bad behavior. With this in mind the Symmetry Principle can be expressed in two propositions R (reward) and P (punishment).

> R. We should reward person S for good act A because S deserves the reward on the basis of A, and, secondarily, rewarding S for A will encourage others to do A-type acts.

> P. We should punish person S for bad act B because S deserves the punishment on the basis of B, and, secondarily, punishing S for A will discourage others from doing B- type acts.

Our theory of desert is primarily retributive, but there is a connection between desert and secondary utilitarian goals. Holding to R and P is likely to produce greater welfare than ignoring them.

Most philosophers accept desert as the necessary criterion for punishment, but some hold that there is a different criterion for distributive justice. One important consequence of the symmetry principle is to rebut this asymmetrical relationship. Since the features of praising and blaming are symmetrical and they form the bases for reward and punishment, it would seem that a strong case for desert exists as the criterion for both punishment and reward.

Other candidates as criteria for justice are ruled out by the symmetry principle. Some philosophers hold that everyone should receive equal amounts of the society's resources. If the symmetry principle is correct, this is not so, since some people may not deserve benefits or punishments. Similarly, some philosophers hold that social goods ought to be distributed according to need. But this criterion fails to fit our theory. We would not punish someone, saying that he had a need to be punished, nor would we reward someone on the basis of need. Someone may have a need for $1000 but not deserve it. It seems more accurate to say that our duty of meeting needs is a function of benevolence (or mercy) rather than justice. Furthermore, needs fluctuate according to economic and social conditions, whereas morality is universal and objective.

Other criteria for justice may exist, but as suggested in Chapter 3, desert is central and if we think it is the dominant criterion in punishment, the symmetry principle shows that it should also be the dominant criterion in the distribution of rewards.

Notes

1. Immanuel Kant, *The Metaphysics of Morals*, trans. E. Hastie (Edinburgh, 1887; originally published 1779), 155.

2. Mike Royko, quoted in Michael Moore, "The Moral Worth of Retributivism" in *Punishment and Rehabilitation*, ed. Jeffrie G. Murphy, 3rd ed. (Wadsworth, 1995), 98–9.

3. In the following analysis I am indebted to Anthony Flew, "Justification of Punishment," *Philosophy* (1954); Joel Feinberg, "Punishment," *Philosophy of Law*, 2nd ed., eds. Joel

Feinberg and Hyman Gross (Wadsworth, 1980); and Herbert Morris, "Persons and Punishment," *The Monist* 52 (October 1968).

4. H. L. A. Hart, *Punishment and Responsibility* (New York: Oxford University Press, 1968), 234.

5. Immanuel Kant, *The Metaphysics of Morals* (1779), trans. E. Hastie (Edinburgh, 1887): 155–6.

6. Herbert Morris, "Persons and Punishment," in Jeffrie Murphy, ed., *Punishment and Rehabilitation*, Wadsworth Publishing Co. See also Michael Davis, "Harm and Retribution" in *Philosophy & Public Affairs* 15, no. 3 (Summer 1986).

7. Daniel Farrell, "Justification of General Deterrence," *Philosophical Review* 94, no. 3 (July 1985).

8. Henry Sidgwick, *Methods of Ethics* (Hackett Publishing Co.), Book III, Ch 5.

9. Sir James Fitzjames Stephens, *Liberty, Equality, Fraternity* (Cambridge: Cambridge University Press, 1967), 152.

10. Sir James Fitzjames Stephens, *A History of Criminal Law in England* (New York: Macmillan, 1863): 80.

11. Unfortunately, the death penalty may not be used enough in many states to serve this function adequately. If it were applied regularly for heinous crimes, it would better approximate it.

12. Stanley Benn, "Punishment," *The Encyclopedia of Philosophy*, ed. Paul Edwards (New York: Macmillan, 1967), vol 7: 29–35.

13. Anthony Quinton, "Punishment" in *Philosophy, Politics and Society*, ed. P. Laslett, (London) 1959; Stanley Benn and R. S. Peters admit that "If utilitarianism could really be shown to involve punishing the innocent, or a false parade of punishment, or punishment in anticipation of an offense, these criticisms would no doubt be conclusive. They are, however, based on a misconception of what the utilitarian theory is about. We said at the beginning of this chapter that 'punishment' implied in its primary sense, not the inflicting of *any* sort of suffering, but inflicting suffering under certain specified conditions, one of which was that it must be for a breach of a rule" ("The Utilitarian Case for Deterrence," 98).

14. Karl Menninger, *The Crime of Punishment* (New York: Viking Press, 1968), 17, 10–11. The passage is remarkable for its apparent contradiction, both denying and asserting the objective reality of justice.

15. Benjamin Karpman, "Criminal Psychodynamics," *Journal of Criminal Law and Criminology*, 47 (1956): 9. See also B. F. Skinner, *Science and Human Behavior* (New York: Macmillan, 1953), 182–93.

16. For a fuller discussion of these issues see my book, *The Death Penalty: For and Against* (Boston: Rowman & Littlefield, 1998), written with Jeffrey Reiman.

17. John Rawls, "Two Concepts of Justice," *Philosophical Review* (1955).

18. Analogues to the karmic principle are found in the Hebrew Bible (Ps 1) and the New Testament (Gal. 6:8 "Whatsoever a man sow that shall he also reap"). George Homans in *Social Behavior: Its Elementary Forms* (London: Routledge & Kegan Paul, 1961), p. 246, argues that virtually every culture examined by anthropologists includes such a principle.

Conclusion

Let justice roll down like waters, and righteousness like an ever-flowing stream.

Amos 5:24

We have examined several classic and contemporary theories of justice, ranging from the ancient desert theory to contemporary libertarian, welfare liberal and pluralistic theories. We have examined the ideas of equal opportunity, retributive justice, and global justice. We have shown the strengths and weakness in each theory. The libertarian theory rightly values liberty and the right to own property, but it neglects other values, such as human need and whether the rich deserve their wealth. The liberal theory rightly focuses on human need and fairness, but neglects desert and merit. The classic theory of desert accords with our reflective intuitions that people should be held responsible for their actions and rewarded according to whether they are good or bad. It comes the closest to being an ideal theory of justice, though it is often difficult, if not impossible, to apply. The desert theory has the advantage that it fits in with our common-sense intuitions and is symmetrical between distributive and retributive justice. The complex pluralist theory of justice should best be seen as a supplement to the classic theory, showing that justice is applied differently in different social spheres, depending on the internal logic of that sphere, though a certain objective core morality must be observed in any social construct.

But justice may be Janus-faced—looking both backward and forward at the same time. We have argued that the liberal theory that focuses on meeting basic needs can supplement the desert theory. If the concept of desert is the conservative aspect of justice, backward looking, the concept of need is the liberal or forward-looking counterpart. What Rawls, Beitz, Shue, and Sterba have done is transform Locke's principle of charity (Chapter 7) into a principle of justice. Rawls's theory is constructive, a theory of fairness that we would all agree on if we were impartial choosers behind the veil of ignorance. Rawls thinks his theory of fairness or institutional desert only applies to societies of moderate scarcity like ours, but Beitz has shown that it can be extended in a cosmopolitan manner to include all people everywhere.

If this is true, then justice has global implications and is an inextricable part of the universal, objective morality, presented in Chapter 1, which will be necessary to build a peaceful and prosperous world. The logic of justice is the logic of cosmopolitanism. We must expand the circle of our concern to include people everywhere without regard to race, religion, ethnicity, or national origin.

We conclude, then, that although a core objective morality underlies the application of justice, the applications themselves are complex and pluralistic

(Chapter 5), applying to various domains differently. With regard to crime and punishment, desert is more salient; with regard to community involvement and health care, need is the core value; with regard to economics, contribution is most relevant; and with regard to jobs and offices, merit is the crucial criterion.

What I hope to have shown in this volume is that while there are certain fixed anchors in the concept of justice, such as desert, the application is complex and ever evolving, as the human predicament changes. Philosophically, much work still needs to be done to sort out the conceptual landscape. But we know enough to apply the concept to the world in which we live, with the goal of making this world more just and peaceful.

For Further Reading

Arthur, John, and William Shaw, eds. *Justice and Economic Distribution*. Upper Saddle River, NJ: Prentice Hall, 1978.

Barry, Brian. *The Liberal Theory of Justice*. Oxford: Oxford University Press, 1973.

Barry, Brian. *Justice as Impartiality*. Oxford: Oxford University Press, 1995.

Buchanan, Allen. *Ethics, Efficiency and the Market*. Lanham, MD: Rowman & Allenheld, 1985.

Buchanan, Allen. "Justice as Reciprocity versus Subject-Centered Justice." *Philosophy & Public Affairs*, 19:3 (1990).

Butler, Samuel. *Erewhon*. New York: Modern Library, 1872.

Campbell, Tom. *Justice*. London: Macmillan, 1988.

Christmas, John. *Social and Political Philosophy*. London: Routledge, 2002.

Clayton, Matthew, and Andrew Williams, eds. *The Ideal of Equality*. London: Palgrave Macmillan, 2002.

Darwall, Stephen, ed., *Equal Freedom*. Ann Arbor: University of Michigan Press, 1995.

Dworkin, Ronald. *Law's Empire*. London: Penguin, 1986.

Dworkin, Ronald. *Sovereign Virtue: Theory & Practice of Equality*. Cambridge, MA: Harvard University Press, 2000.

Feinberg, Joel. *Social Philosophy*. Upper Saddle River, NJ: Prentice Hall, 1973.

Gauthier, David. *Morals by Agreement*. Oxford: Oxford University Press, 1986.

Goodman, Lenn E. *On Justice*. New Haven, CT: Yale University Press, 1991.

Gutmann, Amy. *Liberal Equality*. Cambridge: Cambridge University Press, 1980.

Hare, R. M. "Justice and Equality." In *Justice and Economic Distribution*, eds. John Arthur and William H. Shaw. Upper Saddle River, NJ: Prentice Hall, 1978.

Hobbes, Thomas. *Leviathan* (first published in 1651). London: Penguin, 1968.

Kershnar, Stephen. *Desert, Retribution and Torture*. Lanham, MD: University of America Press, 2001.

Mill, John Stuart. *Utilitarianism* (first published in 1863). Indianapolis: Hackett Publishing Co., 1979.

Miller, David. *Social Justice*. Oxford: Oxford University Press, 1973.

Murphy, Jeffrie G., ed., *Punishment and Rehabilitation*. Belmont, CA: Wadsworth Publishing Co., 1995.

Murray, Charles. *Losing Ground*. New York: Basic Books, 1984.

Narveson, Jan. *Respecting Persons in Theory and Practice*. Lanham, MD: Rowman & Littlefield, 2002.

Nathanson, Stephen. *Economic Justice*. Upper Saddle River, NJ: Prentice Hall, 1998.

Norman, Richard. *Free and Equal*. Oxford: Oxford University Press, 1987.

Nozick, Robert. *Anarchy, State and Utopia*. New York: Basic Books, 1973.

Okin, Susan. *Justice, Gender and the Family*. New York: Basic Books, 1989.

Pogge, Thomas, ed. *Global Justice*. Oxford: Blackwell, 2001.

Pojman, Louis P. *Ethics: Discovering Right and Wrong*. Belmont, CA: Wadsworth Publishing Co., 1994.

Pojman, Louis P., ed. *Modern and Contemporary Political Philosophy*. New York: McGraw-Hill, 2002.

Pojman, Louis P., and Owen McLeod, eds. *What Do We Deserve?* Oxford: Oxford University Press, 1998.

Pojman, Louis P., and Robert Westmoreland, eds. *Equality*. Oxford: Oxford University Press, 1997.

Rakowski, E. *Equal Justice*. Oxford: Oxford University Press, 1991.

Raphael, D. D. "Conservative and Prosthetic Justice." *Political Studies* 12 (1964).

Raphael, D. D. *The Concepts of Justice*. Oxford: Oxford University Press, 2001.

Rawls, John. *A Theory of Justice*. Cambridge, MA: Harvard University Press, 1971.

Rawls, John. *Political Liberalism*. Cambridge, MA: Harvard University Press, 1993.

Reiman, Jeffrey. *Justice & Modern Moral Philosophy*. New Haven, CT: Yale University Press, 1990.

Reiman, Jeffrey, and Louis Pojman. *The Death Penalty: For and Against*. Lanham, MD: Rowman and Littlefield, 1998.

Rescher, Nicholas. *Distributive Justice*. Indianapolis, IN: Bobbs-Merrill, 1966.

Rescher, Nicholas. *Fairness: Theory & Practice of Distributive Justice*. New Brunswick, NJ: Transaction Publishers, 2002.

Roemer, J. *Theories of Distributive Justice*. Cambridge, MA: Harvard University Press, 1996.

Sadurski, W. *Giving Justice Its Due*. Dordrecht: Reidel, 1985.

Sandel, Michael. *Liberalism and the Limits of Justice*. New York: Cambridge University Press, 1982.

Sen, A. K. *Inequality Reexamined*. Oxford: Oxford University Press, 1992.

Sher, George. *Desert*. Princeton, NJ: Princeton University Press, 1986.

Sidgwick, Henry. *The Methods of Ethics*. London: Macmillan, 1907.

Singer, Peter. *One World*. New Haven, CT: Yale University Press, 2002.

Solomon, Robert, and Mark Murphy, eds. *What Is Justice?* Oxford: Oxford University Press, 1990.

Shaw, William. *Contemporary Ethics: Taking Account of Utilitarianism*. London: Blackwell, 1999.

Sterba, James P. *How to Make People Just*. Lanham, MD: Rowman & Littlefield, 1988.

Sterba, James P. *Justice for Here and Now*. New York: Cambridge University Press, 1998.

Sterba, James P., ed. *Justice: Alternative Perspectives*. Belmont, CA: Wadsworth Publishing Co., 2003.

Temkin, Larry. *Inequality*. Oxford: Oxford University Press, 1993.

Waldron, Jeremy. *The Right to Private Property*. Oxford: Oxford University Press, 1988.

Walzer, Michael. *Spheres of Justice*. New York: Basic Books, 1983.

Wolgast, Elizabeth. *The Grammar of Justice*. Ithaca, NY: Cornell University Press, 1987.

Young, Iris. *Justice and the Politics of Difference*. Princeton, NJ: Princeton University Press, 1990.

Index